GETTING TO KNOW THE

HEART OF GOD

A Study of Hebrews, Chapters 5-10

by Eva Gibson

DISCOVERING *the* Heart of God SERIES

A Bible Study

AGLOW®
Women's Aglow Fellowship International
P.O. Box 1548
Lynnwood, WA 98046-1548
USA

Cover design by Paz Design Group

Women's Aglow Fellowship International, is an interdenominational organization of Christian women. Our mission is to lead women to Jesus Christ and provide opportunity for Christian women to grow in their faith and minister to others.

Our publications are used to help women find a personal relationship with Jesus Christ, to enhance growth in their Christian experience, and to help them recognize their roles and relationship according to Scripture.

For more information about our organization, please write to Women's Aglow Fellowship International, P.O. Box 1548, Lynnwood, WA 98046-1548, USA, or call (206) 775-7282.

Unless otherwise noted all Scripture quotations are from the New King James Version (NKJV). Copyright ©1979, 1980, 1982, Thomas Nelson, Inc. Other versions are abbreviated as follows: New American Standard Bible (NASB), New International Version (NIV), The Amplified Bible (TAB), and The Living Bible (TLB).

ISBN 1-56616-010-3

1 2 3 4 5 Printing/Year 97 96 95 94

AGLOW BIBLE STUDIES

Basic Series

God's Daughter
Practical Aspects of a Christian Woman's Life

The Holy Spirit and His Gifts
A Study of the Spiritual Gifts

Coming Alive in the Spirit
The Spirit-Led Life

Discovering the Heart of God Series

Called to Spiritual Maturity
A Study of Hebrews, Chapters 1-4

Getting to Know the Heart of God
A Study of Hebrews, Chapters 5-10

Practicing Truth in the Family of God
A Study of Hebrews, Chapters 11-13

Write for a free catalog

*Write or fax for a Leader's Guide
(See page 141 of this study)*

Dedicated to

all those who believed in me.

Expecially my mother
Jenny Nickerson
and my brother,
Dale.

A special thank you to
Karen Anderson, Aglow editor.
She partnered with Jesus in interceding for me.

Contents

Editor's Note

Thank you for your words of encouragement about Aglow's Bible study series on Hebrews, and for your constructive suggestions about making it easier for group study.

We are thankful that many of you like this study because it's about maturing in Christ. You tell us it challenges you to spend time building intimacy with Jesus, a commitment that blesses Father God's heart.

Some of you expressed dismay because each lesson took more time than you could offer. It is not God's desire to burden or weary us in seeking intimacy with Him. Yet, true intimacy takes time for involvement. There are no fill-in-the-blank shortcuts to relationship.

Our lives leave precious little time to seek His face.

Are you working women who study together one night a week? Are you mothers with small children who squeeze out one precious hour to meet in the morning? Are you already committed to a full calendar of leadership in your church or a community outreach? We trust group leaders to be prayerfully attentive to those needs.

Below are a few suggestions on how to bite into each lesson in smaller mouthfuls.

Finally, we've included a meaningful passage from Dr. Larry Crabb. Because the purpose of this study remains the same, we knew you would take to heart his words on biblical intimacy just as we did.

Some suggestions on how to use this study:

Author Eva Gibson (see Introduction), offers general suggestions on how to use this book, based on each four-part study. Following are suggestions for breaking each study into smaller parts.

1. *God Speaks* inductive study questions can be studied in two or more meetings rather than one.
2. *I Listen* journaling suggestion can be assigned, with one or two women completing one question each. The women who choose to journal more questions are free to do so.
3. One day's suggestion (of five) on prayer in *We Talk Together* can be chosen by the leader for a time of prayer during the meeting.
4. The passage in *Walking Along Together* can be read aloud by a volunteer either at the beginning or end of the meeting. That way, those who have been unable to read the passage for themselves, will hear its message.

Because we are passionate people terrified of isolation, God's Word to us must be understood and embraced and shared with a passion stronger than all others.

But that rarely happens. In our culture, training in the Bible is too often dull. We tend to be precise but boring.

. . . We have managed to take the only really living Book and squeeze the life out of it with an exacting exegesis that engages the brain but not the relationship-starved soul, and then we arrange the remaining dust into neat little piles that we call theology—the study of God. How utterly terrible!

. . . We must learn to see God as the only Person who can relieve the terror of isolation with His powerful and good presence, the only One who can melt our determination to survive isolation by enticing us with the joys of involvement.[1]

—Larry Crabb
Founder and Director,
The Institute for
Biblical Counseling

---

1. Larry Crabb, *Who We Are & How We Relate,* The Institute of Biblical Counseling Series leader's guide (Colorado Springs, CO: NavPress, 1992), pp. 25-27.

Introduction

Ever since I was a little girl, the concept of Jesus as the Shepherd captured me. Maybe it was because of the sheep in our pasture. I loved following the tiny trails they made in the woods, and the first animal I ever claimed as my own was the lamb I named Curley T.T.

Although I never knew a shepherd, I saw myself as a lamb being carried in the Shepherd's arms. Even now this picture of my Lord touches the deep places of my heart. It's a truth that's walked with me ever since.

Not so the concept of Jesus as my Great High Priest.

Priests were unknowable I thought. So were tabernacles and offerings and altars. None of these fit into my understanding of God at all, at least not for a long time.

Then I began studying the book of Hebrews. The first four chapters were a call to spiritual maturity. Chapters 5-10 continued that call. But something else came through the pages. Something beautiful.

Something precious that I was only beginning to understand. Jesus as the Great High Priest was capturing my heart. Not only was He capturing it, He was softening it, shaping it into a reflection of His own.

I know now that we can't grow in maturity unless we understand the heart of God. Nor can our hearts stay soft without frequent reminders of Jesus' sacrifice for sin. Seeing Jesus as the compassionate priest who enters our sorrows and struggles not only gives us power, it keeps us tender. It helps us persevere.

The writer of Hebrews knew what it could do for the Christians undergoing persecution. He told his readers, "We have much to say about this [Jesus as our eternal High Priest], but it is hard to explain because you are slow to learn" (Heb. 5:11 NIV).

Did the the human author of Hebrews realize how hard it would be for today's woman to understand how sacrifices and blood and tabernacles can transform her lifestyle? Probably not. But God the divine author knew.

The Old Testament priesthood gives us some of the richest teaching about Jesus Christ. It teaches us how to worship, to come near to our living God. To come near to one another.

Let us draw near to His throne. Let's look into the heart of our God and discover more about who Jesus is.

Let's do it together.

How to Use This Book:
This study is designed to help you grow in your understanding of the heart of God. Each study is in four parts:

1. *God Speaks* is an inductive study.

2. *I Listen* has suggestions adapted to journaling to help you apply the truth you're learning to specific areas in your life.

3. *I Worship Him* has encouragment and suggestions for prayer and praise.

4. *Walking Along Together* shows how God made each week's scripture passage real to the author.

The study is designed to be done a little each day, five days a week. You will profit most if you take the time to daily ask the Holy Spirit to be your teacher before you begin.

Since our unfamiliarity with the Old Testament high priestly system causes us to miss a lot when it comes to understanding the significance of Christ as our Great High Priest, we'll need to go back into the Old Testament. We'll be doing that a little at a time throughout this study.

Use each day's study questions to work through the scripture passage. They will prepare you to make daily application in the *I Listen* and help you present your praise and prayers to God in *I Worship Him* with deepened insight. The narrative section is to be read at the end of the week after you have completed all five sections.

You will need this study guide, the NKJV Bible translation, a notebook, and/or your journal, dictionary, and concordance.

It would be good to have a commentary, Bible dictionary and several Bible translations.

If you're part of a group, you'll find it most helpful to complete the study questions before you meet. Solidify what you're learning by being ready to share what you've learned and how it applies to your life. Write down any unanswered questions you may have. Your leader or others in the group may be able to help you further.

For Leaders, A Guide

The book of Hebrews is written to women whom God wants to draw into a deeper relationship with Himself. Women who have problems, women who want more but aren't quite sure what it is they're looking for. Women who want to reflect the heart of God.

Although Hebrews is difficult to understand, it is also filled with some of the richest teaching about our Lord Jesus Christ.

You've taken a giant step in Christian maturity by choosing to study it.

1
...

Our Compassionate High Priest

Hebrews 2:1-3:1, 4:14-5:10

❦ **DAY 1** ❦

GOD SPEAKS

INTRODUCING OUR GREAT HIGH PRIEST

Read **Hebrews 2:17-3:1.**

1. Has a friend ever showed you a photograph of someone you've never met? Someone who was important to her? What details did you observe about the person in the photograph that made it possible for you to recognize her when you saw her?

_____

Getting to Know the Heart of God

God painted a portrait of Christ 1,500 years before He was a born as a human baby in Bethlehem. Louis T. Talbot in his book, *Christ in the Tabernacle,* writes, "If all men of this Christian era would only study the New Testament in the light of the Old, they would look with wonder and awe upon the portrait of Christ in the Old Testament; for it is a true likeness of the suffering, risen, interceding, and reigning Lord Jesus."[1]

In one of the most beautiful portraits ever, God painted Jesus' likeness in the tabernacle and in the priests who ministered there. In Exodus 28, Aaron the high priest, is clothed by Moses for his first sitting. A turban for glory and for beauty is wrapped around his head, a fine linen garment reaches to his feet.

Other costly and beautiful articles of clothing are an embroidered linen coat and a girdle of intricate needlework. The blue robe of the ephod has been ornamented with golden bells and pomegranates embroidered in blue, purple and scarlet. Other details are too numerous to mention here—laces of blue, rings of gold, precious stones adorning the breastplate. Yet each one speaks truth that points to Jesus Christ as the altogether lovely one.

Even the setting—the tabernacle itself—whispers grace and glory. Scholars have noted that the very pieces of furniture in the tabernacle were arranged in the form of a cross. The candlesticks, the table of showbread, the ark of the covenant, all point to Jesus.

That our Lord Jesus ministered as Israel's perfect High Priest and is still ministering to us today is the very heart of the book of Hebrews. Over and over we read that He offered Himself, "once for all" as our sacrifice for sin. We read that He "lives to make intercession" for us at the throne, that He is seated "at the right hand of the Majesty on High."

If only the Jewish leaders had studied His portrait in the Old Testament, they would have recognized their Messiah when He came. As it was, they crucified the very One they waited for.

2. As we read and studied Hebrews 1-4, in the first of this Bible study series, *Called to Spiritual Maturity,* we saw Jesus as the divine Son of God. We also glimpsed His humanity—He is our brother, our great High Priest. We're going to more fully explore Jesus' humanity in Hebrews 5-10. In order to do that we need to go back into the first four chapters. Jesus is first called a High Priest in Hebrews 2:17.

16

Read **Hebrews 2:14-18.**
What two adjectives describe the high priest in verse 17?

_____

What do they mean to you?

_____

3. When we carefully observe someone, we learn more about who he is. When we observe someone supremely great and discover more facets of his greatness—the more we understand his heart. Why might this be particularly important in our relationship with God?

    _____

    a. Respond to this statement with your heart: The purpose of the priesthood was to teach the people that atonement for sins required an innocent victim to die and shed its blood before a sinner could go free.
        The *NIV Study Bible* footnote says: "In order for Christ to turn aside the wrath of God against guilty sinners, He had to become one with them and die as a substitute for them."[2]

    b. List as many truths as you can find in these verses to show what Jesus had to be and do in order to free us from sin.

        _____

        _____

    c. What words and phrases about Christ's humanity pull hardest at your heart?

        _____

    d. What words and phrases about your own humanity can you relate to?

        _____

17

e. Why is it easier to learn from someone who has experienced some of the same things you're experiencing?

_____

4. Read **Hebrews 3:1** in several translations. What important command is given here?

_____

When we fix our attention on Jesus in this verse we see Him as both A_____ and H_____ P_____. What does the writer mean when He calls Jesus an apostle? The Greek word *apostolos* means one who is sent forth. Jesus came from God, clothed with God's power. In Him God speaks. When we listen to Him we hear God's voice.

That Jesus is also the Great High Priest recurs again and again in the book of Hebrews. Read the following quotation from William Barclay:

> The priest is the person who builds a bridge between man and God. To do that he must know both man and God. He must be able to speak to God for men and to speak to men for God. Jesus is the perfect High Priest because He is perfectly man and perfectly God; He can represent man to God and God to man. He is the one person through whom man comes to God and God comes to man.[3]

> Which of these two titles in 3:1 are most meaningful to you right now? Explain why in one or two sentences.

_____

_____

5. One of the ways we fix our attention on Jesus is through reading the Word of God. However, Jesus as our High Priest held more meaning for the believers who received the letter to the Hebrews than it does for us today. Our unfamiliarity with the Old

Testament high priestly system causes us to miss a lot when it comes to understanding the significance of this title. Therefore, if we're truly going to understand the heart of God as revealed in the book of Hebrews, we're going to need to go into the Old Testament from time to time.

6. Read **Exodus 28.**
   Each article of clothing the high priest wore had a special significance that can help us better understand the high priest's ministry. As you read, note details you especially enjoy.

   _____

   _____

I LISTEN (Journaling Suggestion)
   Jot down some practical things women can do that will help them fix their thoughts on Jesus: e.g. Write a verse on a file card and put it by the kitchen sink. Remind a child that Jesus loves him. Tell a friend what you discovered about Him.
   Plan to share your ideas with your Bible study group next week.

I WORSHIP HIM (Praise)
   Acknowledge the beauty of Christ's presence in your life by praising Him for being your merciful and faithful High Priest, the Altogether Lovely One, the Fairest of Ten Thousand.

❦ DAY 2 ❦

GOD SPEAKS

JESUS OUR MEDIATOR

Read **Hebrews 4:14-16.**
1. Have you ever felt like you needed someone to take your part? A lawyer maybe. One who cared about you and was ready to take the stand on your behalf? Even fight for you?
   Describe what you think this person could do for you.

_____

_____

Read **Job 9:32-33.**

2. Job was a man who lived long before Jesus came into the world as a human baby. He even lived before Moses and the priests. Just what exactly is the longing of Job's heart? Paraphrase it into your own words. (When we paraphrase scripture it becomes more truly our own.)

_____

_____

3. Later God appointed Moses as a mediator for the children of Israel. What do you see Moses doing in **Exodus 24:1-8; 32:11-14**?

_____

_____

4. In **Exodus 28:9-12** God charged Aaron the high priest to bear the names of the sons of Israel over his heart when he entered the Most Holy Place behind the curtain. What happened to the curtain when Jesus died on the cross (**Mark 15:37-39**)? Why is this significant for us?

_____

_____

Read **Hebrews 4:14-16** again.

5. That Jesus is our mediator who is even now in heaven at the right hand of God interceding for us is a momentous truth, one that we need to fix our thoughts on. Writing down two or three of your observations from each of the following New Testament scriptures will help you do this.

Romans 8:34 _____

1 Timothy 2:5 _____

Hebrews 7:23-25 _____

Hebrews 10:19-23 _____

I LISTEN

How does it make you feel to know that you—if you are a child of God—can come directly into God's presence at any time? That you can approach God's throne with confidence, knowing you will receive the mercy and grace you need?

I WORSHIP HIM

Just as Aaron bore the Israelites' names on his heart, so does Jesus bear your name before the heavenly Father. Praise Him now for being your Lawyer, your Mediator, Your Advocate.

Worship Him in the beauty of His holiness.

❧ DAY 3 ❧

GOD SPEAKS

PERFECT PRIEST, POWERFUL KING

Read **Hebrews 5:1-10.**
1. What qualifications would you want someone to have who was going to represent you in the Supreme Court of the United States? What would you want him to do for you?

_____

_____

2. God has laid out certain important qualifications for a priest in His Word. The writer of Hebrews lists three of these in

21

Getting to Know the Heart of God

Hebrews 5:1-4. What are they?

a. (vv. 1-2) _____

b. (v. 3) _____

c. (v. 4) _____

God also expected a priest to perform certain responsibilities. List the ones you find in these verses:

The writer of Hebrews gives _____ (v. 4) as an example of a priest. Read about his ordination in **Exodus 28:1-3, 43**. Who is he to minister to?

_____

What could happen to a priest if he didn't obey all the details laid out for him?

_____

Being a priest was serious business. A priest could lose his life if he didn't obey the rules. It was also sacred. A priest ministered to God on behalf of the people. A high priest held the highest office in the Hebrew nation. Even the king wasn't allowed to perform the duties of a priest.

3. What three words in **Hebrews 5:5** connect Jesus Christ to the Old Testament high priest (**Hebrews 5:4**)?

_____

This connective compares Jesus to Aaron. Complete the following sentences:
Aaron was appointed by God from the tribe of Levi; Jesus came as God's own S_____ from heaven, God's P_____ F_____ (5:5-6). Aaron was a sinner while Jesus was p_____ (5:9), without sin. Aaron's mediation was only temporary, Jesus gives e_____ s_____ .

22

4. We learn even more about the superiority of Jesus' priesthood in **5:1-10**. The Old Testament character, _____, is introduced for the first time in verse 6. We'll be looking closer at him later in our study. But right now, we'll look at two facts:
   a. Melchizedek is the only person in the Old Testament who appeared as both a king and a priest.
   b. In this verse Jesus is also introduced as both King and Priest (The writer is quoting from Psalm 110).

Read **Psalm 110**.
How do you see Jesus in this psalm?

_____

_____

I LISTEN

If the Jews had paid greater attention to the Old Testament scriptures they would have seen the portrait of their Messiah. Zechariah even wrote about the two offices of Priest and King that the Messiah would hold. Read **Zechariah 6:9-13**.

How does it make you feel to realize that the priest who's representing you to God is also a king? A King with power to help you? One Who's always there, always available?

What do you need most right now? A compassionate high priest? A powerful king? Bring your needs directly to Jesus as either your High Priest or your King. You might even want to combine the two titles as you talk to Him.

I WORSHIP HIM

Jesus isn't just a King. He's a tender compassionate Priest who longs to be intimately involved in your life. Praise Him today as your gentle High Priest, your powerful King.

❦ DAY 4 ❦

GOD SPEAKS

OUR COMPASSIONATE HIGH PRIEST

Read **Hebrews 5:1-10.**

A little girl was given a picture of a cross to color. Instead she drew a crown at the top of the cross. She got out sparkles and vari-colored bits of plastic to decorate it. After she'd happily glued and colored she sat back to view her creation. A moment later she reached for the scissors.

"I don't want the cross," she said. "I only want the crown."

1. Have you ever felt like this little girl? Tell of a time in your life when you avoided something hard, something that might have been painful and reached instead for that which was easy. Or pretty. Or just plain fun.

   _____

   _____

2. Read **Luke 19:29-40.**
   Before Jesus died on the cross, he entered Jerusalem as a King. How would you describe the mood of the disciples as they unloosed the colt and brought it to Jesus?

   _____

   How would you describe the mood of the multitude of disciples?

   _____

   The mood of the Pharisees?

   _____

   Of Jesus Himself?

Read **Luke 19:41-44** and **22:39-44.**

3.   How would you describe Jesus' heart for people as revealed in these accounts?

Compare **Luke 22:39-44** with **Hebrews 5:7-9**. Write down words and phrases that describe the agony Jesus experienced.

How does it make you feel to realize that Jesus' agony was so great that His sweat turned to blood?

Read **Hebrews 5:7-8** in other translations. For example *The Amplified Bible* says, "In the days of His flesh [Jesus] offered up definite, special petitions [for that which He not only wanted but needed], and supplications, with strong crying and tears, to Him Who was[always] able to save Him [out] from death, and He was heard because of His reverence toward God—His godly fear, His piety [that is, in that He shrank from the horrors of separation from the bright presence of the Father]. Although He was a Son, He learned [active, special] obedience through what He suffered."

Read **Luke 23:44-46.**

4.   Is the thought that Jesus, when He was in Gethsemane, may have been anticipating the horror of great darkness that would descend over all the earth when His Father turned away from Him, a new thought to you? How does Jesus' separation from His Father add to the emotion of these verses?

Getting to Know the Heart of God

What can you learn from Jesus' attitude regarding His intense suffering?

_____

What more does it tell you about the heart of God?

_____

I LISTEN

None of us can ever experience the depth of pain Jesus experienced. But have you ever felt an agony so great that it seemed as though your heart was literally broken?

Examine that pain or a crisis you may be facing right now alongside Hebrews 5:7-8. Address your High Priest in a journal entry. If words don't come, simply offer Him your tears. He is your source of comfort. Your powerful High Priest. He understands your pain as no one else can.

I WORSHIP HIM

The name Jesus is Christ's human name. His compassionate name. Worship Him now by calling Him Jesus.

❦ DAY 5 ❦

GOD SPEAKS

LEARNING BY OBEYING

Read Hebrews 5:5-10.

1. Think back over your childhood. How did your parents teach you to obey? How well did you learn obedience?

_____

2. Most of our attention yesterday was on Jesus' suffering in Hebrews 5:7. However, verses 8-10 closely connect with the preceding verse. What punctuation mark is used to end verse 7?

_____

Anytime we see a word or a form of a word recurring in Scripture we need to take note. What word form is found in both verses 8 and 9?

_____

3. Read **Hebrews 5:5-10** again and write down further observations. Two important questions to ask as you observe:
    What names are used for Jesus here?

_____

_____

What do they tell you about Jesus?

_____

_____

It's easiest to understand what someone is saying about someone else when we understand the meaning of key words. Look up *eternal* and *salvation* (v. 9) in a dictionary. Condense the definitions into a sentence or two.

_____

_____

4. Since Jesus was God incarnate, why would He have to learn obedience? The following footnote in the *NIV Study Bible* helps us understand:

Though he was the eternal Son of God, it was necessary for him as the incarnate Son to learn obedience—not that he was ever disobedient, but that he was called on to obey to an extent he had never before experienced. The temptations he faced were real and the battle for victory was difficult, but where Adam failed and fell, Jesus resisted and prevailed. His humanity was thereby completed, "made perfect" (v. 9), and on the basis of this perfection he could become the "source of eternal salvation" (see 9:12).[4]

How is the obedience Jesus learned different from the obedience you learned or are in the process of learning?

_____

_____

Read **Hebrews 9:12-14.**
5.　What perfection do you glimpse in verse 12?

_____

That the one who learned to obey brought salvation to those who obey is an awesome thought. What does Christ's cleansing (**vv. 13-14**) free us to do?

_____

6.　Our study this week concludes with a verse that once again refers to the mysterious Melchizedek. That his priesthood foreshadows Christ's priesthood holds deep truth that's hard to understand. So have some of the other truths we've been considering—Jesus' prayers and cries and tears, His learning obedience through suffering aren't easy to grasp.

It's interesting to note that we aren't the only ones who've struggled. The original readers struggled too. In fact some scholars think **Hebrews 5:11** is a concluding sentence rather than the beginning sentence of a new thought.

What do you think?

_____

Challenge activity: Read **Hebrews 3-10.** Underline the words *priest, high priest, priesthood* and *great priest* whenever they occur. How many did you find?

I LISTEN

Has God spoken to you through His humanity? How can these verses imprint your life? Help you to persevere, even when you're hurting? Choose one of the phrases describing Jesus and incorporate it into a prayer song addressed to Him. Allow your song to communicate your confidence that He is there, ready to share your innermost needs, whatever they may be.

I WORSHIP HIM

When Jesus offered Himself to God as the sacrifice for sins, He became the source of your eternal salvation. Let your praise and worship reflect this truth right now.

WALKING ALONG TOGETHER

I stare at my computer—his name is Mackey John—and he stares back at me. No words pass between us. No thoughts. No ideas. Nothing.

I push the off button. Mackey John's face fades into oblivion as I pick up my Bible and notebook and slip out the door.

Behind my house is a trail that leads into the woods. The shadowed moss and tall ferns beckon. I walk deeper into the forest.

A mossy green mound framed by circling vine maple branches invites and I step off the trail. The leaves rustle as I enter the enclosure. A quiet place. A hallowed place. A place where I can talk to my heavenly Father.

"Lord, you've called me to the book of Hebrews for a purpose. I know that. But I have to be honest. I don't know how to write about high priests and sacrifice and offerings."

I sit down on the mossy mound. My thoughts spin backwards.

When I was a little girl, sheep were pastured here. I remember the tinkling bells and the racing of tiny hooves as I surprised them on the trail. Except the trails were different then, they criss-crossed back and forth through jack fern and hazelnut bushes. Now tall firs grow in their place.

I'm grown now. The sheep are gone. But my Shepherd walks with me. Not so the High Priest.

Getting to Know the Heart of God

I lean back against a branch. I can almost see the child I was—a little girl in a pink dress skipping alongside her Shepherd, her hand tucked inside His. It didn't matter that no one else saw the invisible companion she whispered her thoughts to—"Jesus, my Shepherd, the Lamb of God who takes away the sin of the world."

I bolt upright. That's it. *Just as the Shepherd became the lamb so did the High Priest become the sacrifice.*

I understand something about sacrifice. Long ago God had used Romans 12:1 to draw me to Himself.

A Miserable Teen

The little girl who'd been so drawn to the Shepherd had grown into an unhappy teen. Oh, if only I could be one of the popular girls—a cheer leader who wore green culottes and danced and yelled the teams to victory.

It never happened.

Boys didn't take to me. For one thing I was too tall. No boy wants to date a girl who can stand above him and pat him on the head.

A longing grew inside me. Oh, to be popular with the boys—to have a date every Saturday night.

Later I quit school and went to work in Portland, Oregon. Something happened to me then. Maybe I was a late bloomer or something but all of a sudden the young men began to like me—a date every night—stolen moments in a parked car, a kiss. . . .

I had everything I'd ever dreamed of. Except—it wasn't enough. And that wasn't all. Some of the places we were going, some of the things we were doing weren't right and I knew it.

I walked downtown one day. As I passed by a bookstore with Bibles displayed in the window, I stopped. I went inside, blurted to the woman behind the counter, "Do you ever hire anybody?"

She looked a bit startled. "Usually we have little turnover. But right now we do have an opening. Why don't you fill out an application?"

I did and another woman interviewed me. She seemed interested in my past so I told her about my mother. "But what about you?" she asked. "Do you go to church?"

I shook my head. "I never have. I grew up in the country and my parents never owned a car. But mother made us listen to Brother Jeffries on the radio every Sunday."

I didn't tell her that the preaching and singing hadn't appealed to me. That I hadn't been able to connect church with the Shepherd who'd walked with me on the sheep trails of my childhood, the one who'd sat beside me under our special tree and listened to the thoughts I'd whispered to Him.

Gently the woman said, "We do expect our employees to be part of a local church."

A Glimpse into the Heart of God

The next Sunday found me sitting in a pew. I listened as the pastor began to talk about Jesus' death on the cross. All my life I'd known that Jesus had died for my sins. Now I was seeing it in a new way.

As the man spoke I saw with my heart. I felt the agony of the thorns pressed into His forehead, the horror of the mocking crowds as their spit dribbled off the Shepherd's face. And then they pounded the nail through his ankles. His gasps for breath as He lifted Himself up to speak words of forgiveness tore my heart. When the utter darkness descended I felt a tiny bit of what it must have meant to Jesus to be separated from His heavenly Father.

It was my sin that did it.

The preacher read Romans 12:1: "I beseech you therefore, brethren, by the mercies of God, that ye present your bodies a living sacrifice, holy, acceptable unto God, which is your reasonable service" (KJV).

Then he said, "Isn't it reasonable that this same Jesus who died for you asks you to give your life to Him?"

I leaned forward. *Yes, it is so reasonable, so very reasonable.*

I bowed my head. "Lord Jesus, forgive me for my sins, those sins you died for on the cross. In the best way I know how, I give my life, my body, as a sacrifice to you."

That happened a long time ago but it was the beginning of a new life. And suddenly—sitting there under the vine maple tree I remember—the first book I bought as a new employee at the bookstore was *Christ in the Tabernacle* by Louis T. Talbot. Had God been preparing me even then to write about high priests and sacrifices?

My Sacrifice

I open my Bible. Peter talked about priesthoods and sacrifices, too.

I respond to 1 Peter 2:4-5 by writing in my journal: *"I come to Jesus, the Living Stone. I'm being built into a spiritual house to be a holy priesthood, offering spiritual sacrifices acceptable to God through Jesus Christ."*

In the Old Testament a priest offered sacrifices to God for the people. Had I forgotten that believers today are responsible for sacrifices too?

I turn to Romans 12:1-2: "Therefore, I urge you, brothers, in view of God's mercy, to offer your bodies as living sacrifices, holy and pleasing to God—this is your spiritual act of worship. Do not conform any longer to the pattern of this world, but be transformed by the renewing of your mind. Then you will be able to test and approve what God's will is—his good, pleasing and perfect will" (NIV).

My body, ready to learn obedience, my mind, ready to do His will. . . . My eye jumps across the page (vv. 9-21). I write: *"Ready to be . . .*

. . . devoted to one another in brotherly love,

. . . joyful in hope,

. . . patient in affliction,

. . . faithful in prayer. . . ."

Thoughts from my study in Hebrews 5 color the words before me. *"Lord Jesus, sacrifice is close to Your heart and sacrifice always costs somebody something. Even David said, 'I won't sacrifice to you that which cost me nothing.'*

"Your sacrifice cost You Your life, Your blood. . . .

"Gentle Shepherd, merciful High Priest, I love You. I want to learn obedience—and right now that means writing—when words don't come. It means keeping on—when friends are off having coffee and I have to stay home and look at Mackey John."

I stand up, brush twigs and moss off my jeans. Today my writing is my sacrifice, my spiritual act of worship.

2
...
Don't Quit—
Keep Persevering

Hebrews 5:11-6:12

❦ DAY 1 ❦

GOD SPEAKS

A CALL TO GROW UP

Read Hebrews 5:11-14.
1. Were some things especially hard for you to learn when you were a child? An adult? Give an example or two.

   _____

2. Complete the following observations of verses 11-14:
   In v. 11 the writer describes his readers as _____
   In v. 12 teachers are contrasted with those _____

33

Getting to Know the Heart of God

In v. 12 milk is contrasted to _____

In v. 13 the readers are likened to _____

In v. 14 infants are contrasted with _____

Write down three additional observations from the passage. Look for names, pronouns, key words, etc.

_____

_____

Choose one of the key words you selected and look it up in the dictionary. What additional insights do you discover?

_____

3. The writer of Hebrews isn't the only New Testament writer who used milk as a metaphor for elementary instruction in God's Word. Read **1 Corinthians 3:1-2** and **1 Peter 2:2**. How are these verses similar to **Hebrews 5:12-14**?

_____

4. Read **Hebrews 5:14** again. Not only do we grow spiritually as we study God's Word, we also need to apply what we learn. What can we expect God to develop in our lives as result of consistent study and application?

_____

Read **Ephesians 4:13-16**.

5. What happens in the Body of Christ when individuals grow up in the Lord Jesus?

_____

_____

What are some of the things we can expect to happen in our churches as a result of it?

_____

_____

I LISTEN

How would you describe your intake of spiritual "food" (God's Word)? Your exercise program (application of God's Word)? How well do you discern good and evil? Use these questions to evaluate your progress toward spiritual maturity. What weaknesses do you see? What are your strengths? Talk to God about them in your journal.

I WORSHIP HIM

Neither physical nor spiritual infants can discern good from evil. But when we become children of God through a personal relationship with Jesus Christ we can know that the Holy Spirit is our teacher!

Read **John 14:25-26**. Spend time praising the Father and Jesus the Son for giving you the Holy Spirit to be your teacher.

❦ DAY 2 ❦

GOD SPEAKS

PRESS ON TO MATURITY

Read **Hebrews 5:11-6:3.**
1. What is your idea of a mature believer? Write a brief description of someone you know who exhibits spiritual maturity. Compare your description to Hebrew 5:14.

    _____

    _____

2. Yesterday we looked at Hebrews **5:11-14**. How would you rate the believer's spiritual development mentioned here on a scale of 1-10?

_____

What three essentials for spiritual growth in verse 14 did you discover?

_____

_____

3. Our major goal as Christians should be to grow up. In **verses 6:1-2** the writer gives his readers some specific instructions. Although they'd taken the first steps toward maturity, they'd slipped back to where they were at the beginning. They were failing to build on the foundation of what they'd been taught.

    Write six important truths listed in these verses on the foundation below.

Pastor and author Charles Swindoll lists three categories included in this foundation—*conversion*—"not laying again the foundation of repentance from dead works and of faith toward God"; *church policy and preferences*—"instructions about washings and laying on of hands"; and *prophecy*—"the resurrection of the dead and eternal judgment."[1]

Why do you think it might be important to get beyond these basic teachings?

_____

_____

4. Read **Hebrews 6:1-3** again. Note the pronouns that the writer uses. Why are they significant?

Faith and repentance are key words in this passage. The *NIV Study Bible* says, "1) *repentance*. That change of mind that causes one to turn away from sin and/or useless rituals. 2) *faith in God*. The counterpart of repentance. As repentance is turning away from the darkness of sin, faith is turning to the light of God."[2]

Look up *repentance* and *faith* in your dictionary. Use what you discover to write a personalized definition of each word.

5. One of the key phrases in these verses is "let us go on...." **Verse 3** sums it up: "This we will do, if God permits." How does this verse and **1 Corinthians 16:7** emphasize dependence on God?

I LISTEN

Faith is more than a mere conviction that there is a God. Faith means trusting in God in a personal relationship. Can you look back at a time in your life when you chose to turn away from your sins and follow Christ? What kind of progress have you made since in your spiritual journey of faith? Write about it in your journal.

If you do not yet have this kind of faith, you are encouraged to read the account of Jesus and the woman at the well in John 4. What is the gift Jesus offers this woman (vv. 10-14). What is her response (v. 15)?

What is the gift that He offers you? What is your response? Write about it in in your journal.

I WORSHIP HIM

Faith is important to the writer of Hebrews—some have even called faith his theme song. Read **Hebrews 11:1-3**. Use one or two of these thoughts to write a simple song of faith. Sing it to Jesus.

❦ DAY 3 ❦

GOD SPEAKS

LEARNING FROM A DIFFICULT PASSAGE

Read Hebrews 6:4-6.

1. What are some things you fear? for yourself? your family? your friends? Do you consider these fears beneficial or harmful? Have you ever felt fear as you read God's Word? What happened in your life as a result of your fears?

    _____

    _____

    _____

2. William Barclay calls Hebrews **6:4-8** one of the most terrible passages in scripture. Hebrews 6:3 transitions us into the heart of this fearsome warning; the one thing that could keep a person from spiritual maturity was falling away.

    Many godly men and women over the ages have come to different conclusions as they've studied this passage. The two most commonly held interpretations are 1) The people addressed here are Christians who are in danger of losing their salvation. 2) The people addressed in this passage are only professing Christians who have been exposed to the gospel but are not truly believers.

    A third interpretation comes from the *Bible Knowledge Commentary.*

    ... that a warning is given of the danger of a Christian moving from a position of true faith and life to the extent of becoming disqualified for further service (1 Cor. 9:27) and for inheriting millennial glory.[3]

    Let's begin our own study by a careful observation of **verses 4-6**. What pronouns does the writer use?

    _____

What words/phrases have been used in other passages to describe Christians? List them.

_____

3. Choose one of these words to look up in your concordance. Has the writer used it in other places? What additional insights did you discover?

_____

_____

Check other references in the New Testament where your selected word appears. What did you learn from these scriptures?

_____

4. We need to pay additional attention to *repentance, renew* and *fall away* in verse 6. What did you discover earlier about the word *repentance*? (Day 2, #4)

_____

_____

That *repentance* means a complete change of mind is further emphasized in this verse with the word *renew. Fall away* implies there is something to fall away from. Even though we can always be forgiven and restored, there can come a time in a believer's life when her heart becomes so hardened that she can't bring herself to turn back to God. The result is that she crucifies Christ afresh and bring shame to His name.

Compare this warning with **Hebrews 10:26.**

_____

Read **1 Corinthians 10:12.**

What do these warnings say to you?

_____

5. In *The Letter to the Hebrews* William Barclay responds to verse 6 with this powerful picture of the cross.

> At the back of the thought of the writer to the Hebrews there is a tremendous conception. He saw the Cross as an event which opened a window into the heart of God. He saw it as showing in a moment of time the suffering love which is for ever in that heart. The Cross said to men: "That is how I have always loved you and always will love you. This is what your sin does to me and always has done to me and always will do to me. This is the only way I can ever redeem you." In God's heart there is always, so long as there is sin, this agony of suffering and redeeming love. Sin does not only break God's law; it breaks his heart. It is true that when we fall away, when we sin, we crucify Christ again.[4]

I LISTEN

Reread William Barclay's response to verse 6 again. Underline words and phrases that create pictures in your mind. Even if you're not an artist, try to draw what you see in a simple illustration in your journal. Ask God to enlighten your mind and heart as you sketch.

I WORSHIP HIM

Praise God for the glimpse of His heart that you've been given today.

❦ DAY 4 ❦

GOD SPEAKS

A PARABLE OF THE EARTH

Read **Hebrews 6:4-8.**
1. Have you ever known someone who turned to Christ, then later

turned away? What happened in her life as a result? What effect did it have on you?

_____

_____

2. Reread **verses 7-8**. Since the words we studied yesterday seem to describe Christians, what are the two crops we're capable of producing? Draw a picture of what you see.

3. Jesus also told a parable about the ground, the seed and the crop. Read about it in **Matthew 13:19-23**. What does He say about the crop produced in the good ground?

_____

4. Reread **Hebrew 6:8**. What three things did the author say about the ground that yields thorns and thistles?

_____

_____

The Greek word for *worthless* is "adokimos" and means, not standing the test, rejected. The same has also been translated "depraved," "disqualified," "fail the test," "rejected," and "unapproved." Underline the word or words that speak most directly to you.

The phrase, *close to being cursed* calls to mind the reader's Jewish background. Moses taught that obedience resulted in temporal blessing, disobedience in temporal cursing (Deut. 28). The unbelieving Exodus generation who failed to possess the land were cursed with hardship and physical death.

5. The New Testament also teaches there is a sin unto physical death. What do **1 Corinthians 5:1-5** and **James 5:19-20** say about it?

_____

_____

6. What does the burning refer to in **verse 8**?

_____

Read **1 Corinthians 3:10-15** and **2 Corinthians 5:10.**
7. What is your conclusion?

_____

I LISTEN

Explore your spiritual productivity in your journal. The following questions will help you evaluate. What evidences of spiritual fruit do you see in your life? What evidence of thorns? What do you need to do to become more fruitful? What is God saying to you right now?

I WORSHIP HIM

Read **John 15:16**. Praise God for choosing you to bear fruit that brings glory to His name.

❦ DAY 5 ❦

GOD SPEAKS

A CALL FOR PERSEVERANCE IN FAITH

Read **Hebrews 6:9-12.**
1. What are some names that you reserve for special people? How can a certain name convey endearment to someone?

_____

2. How does the writer of Hebrews address these Hebrew Christians?

What does his form of address tell you about his feelings for his readers?

These loving words immediately following one of the sternest passages in Hebrews says much about the writer's heart. It's almost as though he's saying, "If I didn't love you so much, I wouldn't have written with such severity."

3. What positive things can you learn about his readers from this passage?

What is the writer confident they will do?

How can these verses encourage you when you're tired or you've lost your zeal or you're just plain discouraged?

4. What work and labor of love have you performed recently that you don't want God to forget?

What reassurance do you find in these verses?

_____

What is the writer's heart desire for his readers (**vv. 11-12**)?

_____

_____

5. Compare the last verse in our study today (**6:12**) to the first verse we studied in this passage (**5:11**). What ties the two together?

_____

What have you learned this week that will help you to take an active part in your own spiritual growth?

_____

_____

Challenge Activity: With the help of a commentary or two and/or a study Bible, evaluate further what others have written about Hebrews 6:4-8. Are there points on which you agree? disagree?

Prayerfully bring your questions and/or conclusions to the throne of grace. Recognize that even if you don't fully understand this passage, it's okay. Just as maturity is a process, so is understanding. These processes help us grow in Christ's likeness.

I LISTEN

The writer of Hebrews knew how to speak truth—even when it hurt. He also knew how to lovingly encourage.

Most of us are quick to speak truth but slow to show love. Ask the Holy Spirit to bring to your mind a certain someone, a certain action—a hug, a note, a helpful word—you can do this week. Note it in your journal. Then write a prayer asking Him to help you carry through on what your heart tells you to do.

I WORSHIP HIM

Praise God for the people He's brought into your life—those

who help you stay on track with reproof and warnings—those who encourage you to persevere with loving words, an arm around the shoulder.

WALKING ALONG TOGETHER

Rose Mary had long smooth blonde hair and tanned arms. She always had a thick notebook and three or four heavy books with hard covers weighing down her arms when she got on the bus after school.

Rose Mary was in seventh grade and I was sure she didn't know I existed. Sometimes though I snuck peeks at her. She always sat with one of her big books open on her lap, staring intently at the page. What was it that kept her reading so intently?

Then a miracle happened—at least it seemed a miracle to me. Rose Mary sat down beside me, a timid little third grader who blended rather well—at least I thought so—with the brown bus seat. Not that Rose Mary noticed me—she didn't, at least not at first. She just opened the big blue book on top of her stack and began to read. I leaned forward, craning my neck.

The print was tiny. I scrunched closer.

Rose Mary put her finger on a word and looked at me. "Can you read this?" she asked.

I shook my head. "What kind of book is it?"

Rose Mary swelled with importance. "It's my geography book," she said. She pointed at a sentence. "Do you know what these words say?"

I strained to make sense of the long unfamiliar words marching across the page.

"It's the seven rivers in Europe," she said loftily. "I have to memorize them for tomorrow's test."

I listened in awe as the names of strange rivers rolled off her tongue. How could anyone read words like those, let alone keep them inside her head and write them down at a later time?

That night I announced to my mother that I would never be able to go beyond sixth grade. "It's too hard," I said and tried to explain about Rose Mary and the seven rivers of Europe.

"But honey," Mother said, "seventh grade is four years away and every day between now and then you'll be learning more. When you get there you'll be able to read and understand every bit as much as Rose Mary does right now."

Getting to Know the Heart of God

More About Hebrews 6

Years later I remember the incident I just told you about. I'm in Vienna, Austria, and Wendall, a New Testament theologian, and I are working on a Bible study for Eastern Europe. Our Bibles are open to Hebrews.

"Hebrews 6 is a difficult passage, Eva," Wendall explains. "Few others have had greater impact on our thinking than this fearful warning about falling away and entering into such a spiritual state that it's impossible to be renewed to repentance. Have you done your homework?"

I nod. "Chapter 6 is part of an expository on Christ being greater than any earthly high priest—it actually begins with 4:14. And last week I studied chapter 5. Before that I did a topical study on the rest of God in chapters 3 and 4."

I cup my hands on my chin. "You're right about homework, Wendall. It's been hard for me to begin work on this chapter. I guess I'm afraid I might uncover things I won't be able to interpret in light of other scripture."

"Many godly men have disagreed in their interpretation of this passage. I'm not going to tell you what I think, Eva. Or even what I've learned. Not yet. You need to get on with your own observations.

"Do some word studies. When you get to the burning field, you might want to review what you learned about figurative language. And Eva, it's okay to come to a conclusion and then later, as more evidence presents itself, re-evaluate in light of what you discover. Evaluating, re-evaluating and concluding is a process I want to continue the rest of my life."

He smiles. "It's easy to get so caught up in problem passages that we forget to seek out the heart of the message. Whatever you do, don't lose sight of Jesus Christ as your Great High Priest. There's probably no study in scripture that will teach you more about His holiness and compassion, His sacrifice for our sins."

He touches my shoulder. "Don't lose sight of yourself either. Hang in there. You're doing a good work."

In a Vineyard

Sometimes I think about my summer in Vienna, Austria. So much to learn. So little time to do it in. But how faithful God showed Himself to be. During the day He surrounded me with His special people, Wendall, Phil and Cindy, Debbie, Sylvia, Jan. . . .

In the evening I'd take my Bible and notebook and walk to the vineyards. I'd climb to the top of the hill and, as evening colored the sky a pale rose, I'd read and write.

Sometimes I'd wonder what I was doing there, so far away from family and friends. Then the wind would rise and rustle the grape leaves. The verse I'd chosen so many years ago to be my life verse would whisper in my heart, sometimes off the pages of my Bible: "You did not choose Me, but I chose you and appointed you that you should go and bear fruit, and that your fruit should remain" (John 15:16).

I knew why I was in Vienna. God's Word was reminding me to continue on.

Works of Love

I'm home now and I'm still writing about Hebrews. Today my Lord encourages me as I study: "God is not unjust; he will not forget your work and the love you have shown him as you have helped his people and continue to help them" (Heb. 6:10 NIV). Phrases sparkle at me: "diligence to the very end," "make your hope sure," "[do not] become lazy."

Not only is He encouraging me about the work I'm doing, He's reminding me that I'm surrounded with people who love and help me, who refuse to be lazy, who diligently keep on doing what they know is right in God's sight. I see people from the past and from the present: Mother and Wendall, Pastor Norm and Bill Zipp, Geri Mitch, Sharon Leach, Jane Moad and Kathy Munger, my husband, my children, my editor. They keep coming—so many more—I think I even recognize funny little Rose Mary . Each in his own way has helped me or is helping me grow in spiritual maturity.

Later in my quiet time, the Lord brings Galatians 6:9-10 to my attention. I paraphrase it into words I hear with my heart: *"Eva, do not lose heart in doing good."* I draw a heart with a bent back: *"In due time you shall reap if you do not grow weary."* I drape a heavy load onto my heart's back. *"So then, while you have opportunity, do good to all men, women and children, especially to those who are of the household of faith."*

A house filled with faces and I'm ready to write my response back to Him: *"Just as others have helped me, so also do You want me to do good to others."* I draw a face with wide eyes and a nose like mine. *"A note to Ellen, another to Jan. A special hug for my husband Bud when he doesn't expect it."* What does a hug look like? *"Dinner for Leigh?"*

I smile. This doing good to the household of faith just might have its own reward.

I can hardly wait.

3
...

A Hope That Enters Heaven

Hebrews 6:13-20

❦ **DAY 1** ❦

GOD SPEAKS

ABRAHAM, A MAN TO IMITATE

Read **Hebrews 6:12-17.**
1. How do you feel when you ask God for something to happen—
    then have to wait a long time before He causes it to happen? It
    could even be a request that God confirmed to you by a promise
    in His Word. And now you're waiting. . . .

_____

2. How is Abraham a good illustration of **verse 12**?

49

_____

3. How many times did you read the word *promise* or *promised* in
    verses 12-17?

    _____

    God made more than one promise to Abraham. Read **Genesis
    12:7, 17:5-6, 18:18, 22:16-18.**

    What did God promise Abraham each time?

    12:7 _____

    17:5-6 _____

    18:18 _____

    22:16-18 _____

    How is Genesis **22:16-18** different from the other three?

    _____

    Compare Genesis **22:16-18** to Hebrews **6:13-15**. What additional
    information about God does the writer of Hebrews give us?

    _____

    The promise God made to Abraham that he and Sarah would have
    a son was first made when Sarah was sixty-five and Abraham,
    seventy-five. How long did they have to wait before God fulfilled
    His promise (**Gen. 17:17**)?

    _____

4. Name a situation that has power to make you doubt God.

Read **Romans 4:18-21.**
5. What more can you learn from Abraham, the man who patiently waited?

How can you apply what you've just learned to the situation that you wrote down?

I LISTEN

Often we think of doubt as being negative. But it isn't always—not if it brings us to God's throne. Picture yourself at His throne right now. What will you say to Him? What will He say to you? Write about it in your journal.

I WORSHIP HIM

God didn't have to swear to guarantee the trustworthiness of His Word. But He understood the hearts of men and did it anyway. Praise Him for His Word, that He's always dependable, that He's always there for you.

❦ DAY 2 ❦

GOD SPEAKS

A PROMISE-KEEPING GOD

Read **Hebrews 6:16-18.**
1. How do you feel when someone promises you she'll do something and then doesn't follow through? What words might you use to describe that person?

2. The word _____ in verse 16 changes the subject
   from Abraham to the custom of _____.
   The Jews were quick to swear an oath. They often swore oaths in
   the name of the Lord God or by an object associated with God.
   Always they swore by _____.

One of the definitions of *oath* in Webster's dictionary is a ritualis-
tic declaration, based on an appeal to God or to some revered person
or object, that one will speak the truth, keep a promise, remain
faithful, etc.

Compare the three things in this definition with the way *The
Amplified Bible* describes God as the object of Sarah's faith.

> Because of faith also Sarah herself received physical power
> to conceive a child, even when she was long past the age for
> it, because she considered {God} Who had given her the
> promise, reliable and trustworthy and true to His word (Heb.
> 11:11 TAB).

Webster   Sarah
speak the truth
keep a promise
remain faithful

3. What key principle (a principle is a fundamental truth, law,
   doctrine or motivating force upon which others are based) is the
   writer of Hebrews trying to convey to his readers in **Hebrews
   6:17-18**?

4. God's Word is _____ **(John 17:17)**;
   therefore, when God confirms His promise with an oath, He's
   giving a double guarantee that He will do what He says He will
   do.

Read verse 18 in another translation or paraphrase. *The Living Bible* says: "He has given us both his promise and his oath, two things we can completely count on, for it is impossible for God to tell a lie. Now all those who flee to him to save them can take new courage when they hear such assurances from God; now they can know without doubt that he will give them the salvation he has promised them."

Finish this sentence: God wants me to know for sure that . . .

_____

5. Sarah saw God as reliable, trustworthy and true to His word. In **Hebrews 6:17-18** the writer to the Hebrews sees God as unchangeable in purpose, absolutely true to His Word and a refuge for us to flee to.

What has God shown you about Himself today?

_____

How has it encouraged you?

_____

How can you communicate what you're learning to someone else? a friend in the office, your husband, your neighbor?

_____

I LISTEN

The writer of Hebrews is exhorting you to cling to Jesus, the only one who gives hope. Has God given you a special promise that you can relate to a situation you're facing? Take hold of the hope Jesus is extending to you by writing His promise in your journal. Make it your own by responding to it in a prayer to your promise-keeping God.

I WORSHIP HIM

Christians possess the greatest hope in the world. Praise the Lord for the hope He's given you today.

❦ DAY 3 ❦

GOD SPEAKS

A HOPE THAT ENTERS THE HOLY OF HOLIES

Read Hebrews 6:19-20.

1. Have you ever said, "I hope thus and such will happen"? What kind of hope did you have in mind? Is the biblical use of the word *hope* different from what we generally think of as hope?

    _____

    _____

2. Look up *hope* in both a dictionary and a Bible dictionary. Compare the definitions. What do you discover?

    _____

    _____

3. One writing technique the writer of Hebrews frequently uses is to briefly introduce a topic, then in later verses explain it more fully. He does this with *hope*.

    He introduces *hope* in 6:11. Then, after he establishes the absolute dependability of God's promises in **6:13-17**, he returns to *hope*. What is the significance of *hope* in **verses 18-19**?

    _____

    What kind of word picture is he painting in **verse 19**?

    _____

    How is it similar to **Hebrews 2:1**?

    _____

How is it different?

---

4. An anchor was a symbol of hope in Bible times. In violent storms the sailors would let down their sails and throw an anchor into the sea. The weight of the anchor or anchors would steady the ship and keep it from being beaten to pieces by the waves. It also kept the ship from being driven into a sand bar or a reef. (See **Acts 27:14-44** for a graphic description of a storm at sea).

    The writer to the Hebrews knew about drifting ships and what anchors could do. That's why he used an anchor as a motif of hope. In these verses he's saying, "A Christian possesses the greatest anchor in the world. His anchor is his hope of salvation."

    This anchor is described as both _____ and _____. It gives a woman stability in the deepest part of who she is. It affects her entire life—her will, her mind, her emotions.

5. In **verse 19**, the writer suddenly switches metaphors. A footnote in the *NIV Study Bible* says, "*inner sanctuary behind the curtain.* Whereas the ship's anchor goes down to the ocean bed, the Christian's anchor goes up into the true, heavenly sanctuary, where he is moored to God himself."[1]

    Read the following scriptures: What are some of the things the Hebrew Christians understood about the inner sanctuary behind the curtain?

    Leviticus 16:2, 12 _____

    Luke 23:45 _____

    Hebrews 4:14 _____

Read **Hebrews 6:20.**
5. Jesus has gone ahead of us into heaven. Because He has we have a hope that is sure. Just as Jesus' resurrected body entered heaven, so will our resurrected bodies also enter heaven. This is our hope.

    Put into your own words what it means to you to have this hope.

_____

_____

The writer to the Hebrews is ready now to take up that which he first introduced in Hebrews 5: Jesus is our High Priest forever—a priest in the order of Melchizedek. We'll be learning more about Melchizedek tomorrow.

I LISTEN

Being moored to God Himself at the throne of grace is a glorious concept. Can you put it into a word picture in your journal? You might even be able to draw a picture or a symbol of what you see.

Or design a motif of hope using some of the pictures suggested in this passage (storm, ship, anchor, curtain, high priest, heaven).

I WORSHIP HIM

Hope steadies us to hang on. To persevere. To walk and sing. Try to find the words to the song, "I Have an Anchor" by Priscilla J. Owens. Make her song your words of praise to your Lord.

❦ DAY 4 ❦

GOD SPEAKS

THE MYSTERIOUS MELCHIZEDEK

Read Hebrews 5:6, 10; 6:20–7:3; Genesis 14:17-24.
1. Name a person that a friend told you bits and pieces about for a long time before you met her. What expectations did you have of that unknown person? How did you feel when you finally met her for the first time?

_____

_____

2. Three times now the writer of Hebrews has mentioned the high priest Melchizedek and how he was a type of Jesus (Heb. 5:6, 10; 6:20). (Webster's dictionary defines a type as: a person, thing, or event that represents or symbolizes another, especially another that is to come.)

   The historical account of Abram's meeting with Melchizedek is in Genesis 14:17-24. The occasion leading to this meeting is described in Genesis 14:1ff. Four kings had carried off Lot, Abram's nephew. When Abram received this news he went to Lot's rescue. After he defeated the four kings he arrived in the valley of Shaveh (many scholars believe this to be the Kidron Valley in Jerusalem). Let's reconstruct it in our own minds by carefully observing **Genesis 14:17-24**.

   The two kings who meet Abram on his return from battle were the king of S _____ (Gen. 14:2) and M _____, king of Salem (Jerusalem). King M _____ blessed Abram; the king of Sodom offered him a deal which A _____ refused. What did Abram swear before the LORD God Most High, Creator of heaven and earth (**vv. 22-24**)?

   _____

   Why do you think Abram did this?

   _____

   Prior to the king of Sodom's offer, Abram had been given a blessing by Melchizedek. Write it below:

   _____

   _____

   How was God confirming His original promise to Abram (**Gen. 12:1-3**) through Melchizedek's blessing?

   _____

3. There is something majestic and mysterious about the unexpected appearance of the ancient King Melchizedek. When Abram paid his tithe to him, he acknowledged that Melchizedek was his superior. When he received Melchizedek's blessing (it is always the superior who blesses the inferior), he further acknowledged Melchizedek's supremacy.

     Abram was face to face with one who was his superior.

     What about you? Have you been able to glimpse a little bit of Jesus' glory and majesty through this Old Testament account of Abram's meeting with Melchizedek?

     What truth so far has touched you most deeply? Try to put it into words so that you can share it with your group when you meet.

     _____

     _____

I LISTEN

     There is something beautiful and touching about Melchizedek, Abram's superior, serving him bread and wine. Read **John 13**. How does Melchizedek remind you of Jesus, the Messiah, in this chapter?

I WORSHIP HIM

     Address your worship to Jesus, the Servant-King. Praise Him for giving His body and blood so that you can come boldly to His throne in heaven. His life has made it possible for you to be made in the righteousness of God.

❧ DAY 5 ❧

GOD SPEAKS

THE PSALM OF THE KING-PRIEST

Read **Genesis 14:17-24, Psalm 110.**

1. Earlier in our study this week, we talked about objects that could be used to create a motif of hope. In a way, Melchizedek could be called a motif of hope in that he was a picture of the Messiah who

was to come. Choose an object or two from either the Genesis account or Psalm 110 that could symbolize hope to your own heart.

_____

2. Psalm 110 has been called "The Psalm of the King-Priest." David, the first Israelite king to sit on Melchizedek's throne, wrote that his descendant, the Messiah, would be a priest forever after the order of Melchizedek. Melchizedek preceded Abram, and when David wrote these words he looked beyond the Levitical priesthood to a time when the priesthood would be done away with.

This prophetic psalm has been given unusual prominence in the New Testament. Jesus quoted Psalm 110:1 in Matthew 22:44, Mark 12:35-37, and Luke 20:42-43. It is also quoted in Acts 2:34-35 and Hebrews 1:13. What significance do these quotations hold for you today?

_____

3. The Messiah is even now seated at the Father's right hand. But there's more to come. At the consummation of the ages He comes to make battle with His enemies. What is the adornment of those who accompany Him (**Psalm 110:3**)?

_____

Read **2 Peter 3:10-14.**
4. What kind of persons does He desire us to be?

_____

I LISTEN

The lifting up of the Messiah's head in Psalm 110:7 speaks of His being exalted. Refresh the heart of your Lord today by singing to Him your own personal psalm of exaltation. Reading different translations and/or paraphrases of Psalm 110 will help you put your feelings into words that you can write in your journal.

Getting to Know the Heart of God

I WORSHIP HIM

Worship has a way of making us beautiful. It cleanses, refreshes and gives us hope. Worship the Lord now in the beauty of His holiness.

Challenge Activity: Scholars have noted that there are four impossible things in the book of Hebrews. What are they?

Hebrews 6:4 _____

Hebrews 6:18 _____

Hebrews 10:4 _____

Hebrews 11:6 _____

What encouragement do these verses give you?

_____

What warnings?

_____

WALKING ALONG TOGETHER

Ever since I was a little girl, I've loved Christmas cards. Eagerly I'd pull them out of the envelopes—a lonely shepherd watching his sheep, a country church wrapped in snow, Mary, Joseph, a baby wrapped in swaddling clothes.

My friend, Julie, sent our family a Christmas card this year. I put it with the rest—but my eyes kept being drawn to it. A little angel—her back to me—looked longingly out an arched window made of stone.

Julie didn't know about the hard thing I was experiencing at my church—misunderstandings festering out of sight, the loss of hope, the gradual loss of ministry, but God did. I felt He had something to say to me through Julie's card.

A Christmas Message

The card is plain enough. A window framed with stone, blue sky, three doves circling overhead. A little angel in a yellow gown, hands cupped beneath her chin, leans against the barren sill. One bare foot rests on the other, her blonde hair catches sunshine from the window. She doesn't know that the shadow she's standing on is the shadow of her wings. She doesn't even know she has wings. . . .

Another dove is perched close to her shoulder. I wonder what He's whispering. Is He calling her to stand, to walk, to soar? To realize the longing caught inside her heart? Is He telling her He's there beside her? That all she has to do is fly out to claim the promises she's been given?

From My Journal

After Christmas I put Julie's card inside my journal. Later I write about it:

"Lord, this little angel in her prison reminds me of me. I've longed so to serve you but slowly, one by one, the ministries I once found joy in have been taken from me.

"The three doves circling overhead represent these ministries, the vision You gave me long ago. Even though I know that writing is at the heart of it, teaching, discipling and team ministry are part of it too.

"Right now these three circles are just out of my reach. "Lord, is the dove at my shoulder Your Spirit? Are you telling me You've already given me wings to realize my vision? That I simply need to let go, soar out of my prison and fulfill my destiny?"

A verse whispers through my soul; "Those who wait upon the Lord shall renew their strength. They shall mount up with wings like eagles" (Isa. 40:31).

Wings to Fly

I reach for *The Amplified Bible*: "But those who wait for the Lord — who expect, look for and hope in Him — shall change and renew their strength and power; they shall lift their wings and mount up {close to God} as eagles [mount up to the sun]."

I return to Hebrews 6: The last part of verse 18 sparkles at me; "We who have fled [to Hi]} for refuge might have mighty indwelling strength and strong encouragement to grasp and hold fast the hope appointed for us and set before [us]. [Now] we have this [hope] as a sure and steadfast anchor of the soul—it cannot slip and it cannot break down under whoever steps out upon it—[a hope] that reaches farther and enters into {the very certainty of the Presence} within the veil" (vv. 18-19 TAB).

I know from my study of Hebrews 6 that it's impossible for my God to lie. That His Word is sure even when everything around me shatters and turns to rubble. He's teaching me that He wants me to lean my entire person on Christ. That if I will but wait and endure and have faith His every promise will be fulfilled in me.

A Motif of Hope

Today as I worked on Hebrews 6, I discovered a motif of hope just right for me. I took an anchor from Hebrews 6, a crown from Melchizedek, dew and a jug of water from Psalm 110.

I circled a rainbow overhead in the sky with one end draping earthward. I drew a cross with a crown and a throne inside the circle, suspended an anchor from the bow.

Next I sketched in my little angel from Julie's card. Her dress is still yellow but now her sash is entwined in the rainbow. Dew sparkles her blonde hair. She holds three white doves in her hand and underneath her arm is a jug of water from the brook by the way.

An eagle flies beneath her feet, his outspread wings mounting ever upward, silver glinting off his wings. Jewels stud her sandals. Is it the preparation of the gospel of peace?

I framed my motif in grape leaves and apple blossoms entwined with various fruits and flowers. Underneath I wrote these words from *The Living Bible*: *"Knowing what lies ahead for you, you won't become bored with being a Christian, ... you will be anxious to follow the example of those who receive all that God has promised them because of their strong faith and patience"* (6:12).

I smile. Every first step is a step of hope, a step of faith. Because of the promises in God's Word I can walk. I can run.

My God is a promise-keeping God! I can fly! I can fly!

4
...

A Superior Priest
Hebrews 7:1-28

❦ **DAY 1** ❦

GOD SPEAKS

THE GREATNESS OF MELCHIZEDEK

1. How would you respond if your best friend came to you and told you that she'd had it? She was ready to go back to her old life—Before Christ. What would you say?

_____

_____

Getting to Know the Heart of God

Many of the Hebrew Christians were being persecuted. Tempted to turn back to the Mosaic Law, the Old Covenant, the ceremonial sacrifices.

"Don't," the writer is saying. "What you have now is greater than anything you've ever possessed—Jesus is more excellent than the prophets, the angels and Moses."

Read **Hebrews 6:20, 7:1-10.**

2. The grand theme the author is about to develop in chapter 7 has already been announced in 6:20. What is it?

_____

3. You learned a lot about Melchizedek last week when you examined the historical account in Genesis that the writer of Hebrews refers to in 7:1-10. As you compare the two passages you'll see a close parallel between Jesus and Melchizedek. However, it's hard for us to discern because our world is so different from that of the first century Hebrew Christians. Let's go back to the Old Testament.

Read **Genesis 14:18-20.**

What do you find out about Melchizedek's parentage?

_____

His ancestry?

_____

His birth?

_____

His death?

_____

How does the very absence of this information make Melchizedek a fitting type of Christ?

_____

_____

Read **Hebrews 7:1-10.**
4. Melchizedek was a man of mystery and majesty. What do you find in these verses that prove he was great?

Hebrews 7:4-6a_____

Hebrews 7:6b _____

Hebrews 7:7 _____

Hebrews 7:8-10_____

5. Look up the following verses about Christ and Melchizedek and complete the following:
    Melchizedek foreshadowed Christ as High Priest because . . .

    . . . he was a m _____(Heb. 7:4; 1 Tim. 2:5).

    . . . he was a k _____-p_____
    (Gen. 14:18 with Zech. 6:12-13).

    . . . his name means "The _____ our _____"
    (Jer. 23:5-6) and he was king of Salem (Jerusalem) which means peace (Jer. 33:15-16).

    . . . he had no recorded "b_____(Heb. 7:3;
    John 1:1) or e _____ of life (Rom. 6:9; Heb. 7:7, 23-25).

I LISTEN

There's a certain hard-to-understand quality about Melchizedek's priesthood that can confuse even the finest of Bible scholars. But wait. These verses reveal two names for Jesus that are less complex. The titles, "King of Righteousness" and "King of Peace" teach us more about Jesus Christ.

Getting to Know the Heart of God

Explore one of these names in your journal as you draw near to God.

I WORSHIP HIM

Address Him by the name that sings in tune with the melody in your heart. "King of Righteousness, King of Peace. . . ."

❧ DAY 2 ❧

GOD SPEAKS

THE ROYAL PRIESTHOOD

Read **Hebrews 7:11-17.**
1. Make two lists—one of the things in your life that are destructible, the other of things that are indestructible. Compare the two. Which has the qualities you'd be wisest to build into your life?

    _____

    _____

    _____

2. The question the writer raises in **verse 11** is crucial. For better understanding, rewrite it into your own words.

    _____

    _____

3. What are some of the physical things that a Levitical priest had to abide by in order to be qualified as a priest?
    A. They could be disqualified because of _____
        (**Lev. 21:16-23**).
    B. The ordination ceremony required them to (**Lev. 8**):

        a. _____

b. _____

c. _____

d. _____

Do you think that these observances were guarantees that could keep these priests from later becoming disqualified? Why or why not?

_____

_____

4. Jesus was from the tribe of Judah, not Levi, therefore it was impossible for Him to be a priest according to the Levitical order. What then was His priesthood based on according to **Hebrews 7:16**?

_____

The NIV translation gives us further insight by using the word *indestructible* (v. 16) to describe His life. Look up *destructible* and *indestructible* in a dictionary. What additional insight do you gain?

_____

5. Neither the law nor the priesthood was able to bring maturity into the life of the believer. Nor could either give the believer access to God. Only Jesus could. What are we assured of in **Hebrews 12:1-2**?

_____

In **Hebrews 4:14-16**?

_____

Getting to Know the Heart of God

I LISTEN

The truth the writer communicates over and over again throughout the book of Hebrews is that of access to God's presence. Only Jesus, a priest forever after the order of Melchizedek, could restore the lost fellowship between God and man. There is no greater privilege than that which allows us to come to God as His Friend.

Write a letter to your dearest friend, the Lord Jesus Christ. Thank Him that He has made a way for you to run into the open arms of the Father.

I WORSHIP HIM

Jesus on the cross was the one perfect sacrifice which atones for sin. Bow before Him.

❦ DAY 3 ❦

GOD SPEAKS

THE NEW PRIESTHOOD

Read Hebrews 7:18-25.

1. Have you ever felt at home in someone's presence? What was there about that person that made you feel safe?

   _____

   _____

2. Hebrews **7:18-19** confirms that Jesus could do what the old priesthood could never do. Compare the law with grace in these verses. On the one hand (the law) . . .

   _____

   On the other hand (grace) . . .

   _____

What can we do as a result of God's grace according to verse 19?

_____

How does it make you feel to realize you can now have access to God?

_____

3. Read **verses 18-19** again. The word _annulling_ (v. 18) could also be translated "cancellation" or "wiped out." (The Greek word is _athetesis_, the word used for annulling a treaty, for taking a name off a register, for rendering a law or regulation inoperative.) How did Jesus' priesthood wipe out the sacrificial and ceremonial law? (See **Hebrews 9:26-28**.)

_____

4. Simon J. Kistemaker in his Hebrews commentary introduces **Hebrews 7:20** with these words:

   "The Aaronic priesthood was instituted by divine law; Christ's priesthood by divine oath. A law can be annulled; an oath lasts forever."[1]

   Once again we are reminded that whenever God confirms a statement by an oath, we can be sure that statement is utterly unchangeable. William Barclay writes:

   "It is woven into the very fibre of the universe and must remain forever."[2]

   What assurance then does Christ's priesthood give us (v. 22)?

   _____

5. **Verses 20-25** contain several significant words. Write down five or six of them. Choose one to study in depth. (Look it up in both a dictionary and a concordance.) Ask questions. How is this word

used in other verses in Hebrews? in the New Testament? What significance do you think it holds for the author? What does it mean to me?

I LISTEN

Grappling with unfamiliar words like *oath, surety, covenant* and *uttermost* can make us brain weary. At times like that we need the quiet assurance of phrases like, "draw near to God" and "He ever lives to make intercession for us." Explore these phrases in your journal. Allow them to lead you to the One who gives rest and assurance.

I WORSHIP HIM

The theme of Hebrews is that Jesus is superior. He's able to save forever those who come to Him. Make this superior forever theme the heart of your praise today.

❦ DAY 4 ❦

GOD SPEAKS

INTRODUCING THE NEW COVENANT

Read Hebrews 7:22-25.

1. What does it mean to receive a guarantee with something you just purchased? What assurance does that guarantee give you?

---

2. *Covenant* is an important word to the writer of Hebrews. He uses it in **verse 22** for the first time. (Altogether He uses it 17 times.)

   A covenant is an agreement between two people. The original agreement between Israel and God was that if the Israelites faithfully obeyed the law, they would be able to have access to God, to enter into intimate friendship with Him.

Read **Exodus 24:1-8.**

3. What was the people's response to the Book of the Covenant Moses read to the people?

   _____

   What was the old covenant based on?

   _____

   Why were the priest's sacrifices necessary every time anyone failed to live up to it?

   _____

4. The new covenant (**Jer. 31:33** and **Heb. 8:10**) has two parties, two promises and one implied condition. Who are the two parties?

   _____

   What are the two promises?

   _____

   How does faith (the condition) enter into it?

   _____

5. The old covenant was based on obedience to the law which a

man could easily break. The new covenant is based entirely on love and Jesus' perfect sacrifice. Jesus Himself has become the guarantee of a better covenant.

6. The writer of Hebrews often uses contrast to clarify truth. He does this when he compares the many priests with Christ's eternal priesthood (**Heb. 7:23-24**). Complete these sentences:

The Levitical priests d _____.

Christ lives f _____.

What important conclusion does the writer come to as a result of this observation (Heb. 7:25)?

_____

_____

What does the phrase "able to save to the uttermost" mean to you right now (v. 25)?

_____

_____

I LISTEN

The verb *to save* (sozo) is used in the sense of absolute. The expression *uttermost* (eis to panteles) is used in the New Testament only one other time (Luke 13:11) of the woman who couldn't straighten herself at all.

Do you have a need to bring before the throne? Describe it in your journal. Then picture Jesus Himself at the throne in heaven. He's bringing your need to His Father and your Father. Our God "is able . . . to do, exceedingly abundantly, above all that we ask or think, according to the power that works in us, to Him be glory" (Eph. 3:20-21).

I WORSHIP HIM

Worship your forever priest by calling on His name. Thank Him for His forever salvation.

❦ DAY 5 ❦

GOD SPEAKS

OUR INDESCRIBABLE JESUS

Read Hebrews 7:26-28.
1. Name some character qualities that you would like to have in an intimate friend.

_____

2. Read **verses 26-28** again. How do you think the author felt as he penned these words describing Jesus, our High Priest?

_____

List the characteristics of our Great High Priest as you find them in **verse 26**. Alongside each one list several other scripture references and descriptive phrases as they pertain to Jesus. The cross-references in a study Bible can be of help here. So can a concordance and other translations. One of them is done for you.

a. _____

b. harmless, free from guilt and blame. John 19:4, 6; Acts 13:28.

c. _____

d. _____

e. _____

3. Compare **Leviticus 16:6-19** with **Hebrews 7:27**. How was Jesus' offering different from those of the Levitical priests?

_____

_____

4. As the writer summarizes his teaching on Jesus' eternal priest-hood (v. 28), he demonstrates again that Hebrews is an epistle of contrasts. Examine the structure below:

For	—	but
the law appoints	—	the word of the oath appoints
as high priests men	—	the Son
who have weaknesses	—	who has been perfected forever

5. Complete the following sentences: Jesus is superior because He
is _____, _____,
_____, _____
and _____than the_____(v.26).
He is superior because His sacrifice was _____
(v. 27b). He is superior because He has been the perfected

_____

(v. 28).

I LISTEN

Jesus was the only priest who took the role of the sacrificial lamb. He was the only priest who could. Meditate on Hebrews 9:24-28, 10:11-14; John 1:29 and Isaiah 53:10-12. Draw a picutre of an altar with a lamb as an offering. Above it write: Jesus is the Lamb. Under-neath write a prayer to the Lamb of God who took away the sins of the world.

I WORSHIP HIM

Make the song the living creatures and the elders in heaven sing in Revelation 6:12-14 your hymn of adoration to the Lamb who was the sacrifice.

Challenge Activity: What are some of the things Jesus asks for His followers in John 17?

v. 13 _____

v. 15 _____

v. 17 _____

v. 21 _____

v. 24 _____

Do you think Jesus is praying the same things for you today (Heb. 7:24-25)? Explain.

_____

WALKING ALONG TOGETHER

There's something special about earthly fathers, especially those who show us glimpses of our heavenly Father. I remember my own—Daddy was a first generation Christian. He met Jesus when he was in his late thirties. A couple of years later he married my mother who was at that time an unbeliever.

Two years after their marriage Daddy led Mother to Jesus. Later Mother led two of her sisters to Him. Looking back I realize that Mother was the more verbal of the two. Daddy only had an eighth grade education and I think it was hard for him to put deep thoughts into words. Maybe that was why I always listened when he did have something to say.

"Saved to the 'Uttermost'"

I'll never forget the day he got so excited about the "uttermost." An unearthly joy sparkled in his brown eyes as he came into the back room where I lay curled up on the bed reading.

"Jesus saves to the 'uttermost,'" he exclaimed. "To the 'uttermost'. Do you see? The 'uttermost!'"

The way he said, "uttermost" made me picture a curling wave holding a sailer in its grip. I imagined Jesus leaning down and snatching the man from the foaming sea.

Daddy said it again, "Jesus saves to the 'uttermost.'" The way his tongue rolled around "uttermost" made goose bumps pop up on my arms. All of a sudden I knew that being saved to the "uttermost" meant more than a helpless swimmer being snatched to safety. It meant more, even more than a baby caught out of a crib in a burning house and carried away to safety.

That day I knew "uttermost" wasn't just for this life. "Uttermost" went beyond space and entered eternity. It meant being saved from hell—and punishment, even when you deserved to be punished. "Uttermost" had something to do with being near the very heart of God and it was a glorious nearness.

At Daddy's Bedside

I remembered that day many years later as I stood beside my father's bed at the veteran's hospital in Portland, Oregon. It was eight years since Daddy had recognized me. Even though I'd helped Mother with his care, he didn't know I was his little girl.

But that day—four days before He entered heaven—I saw something in his brown eyes. Was it recognition? I leaned over the railing and took his hand.

"Daddy," I whispered. "It's your Eva Jane."

He smiled, but no words came.

I began to tell him all the things I hadn't been able to tell him during his lost years of darkness and confusion. I told him about my oldest daughter, Beth. "She's engaged to a fine Christian man, Daddy. His name is Alan and he has a shepherd heart." I told him about my first book for teens. "It's called *Melissa*. It'll be published in the spring." I told him about my other children. And all the time he smiled at me.

Then I talked to Him about the Great Shepherd and read the twenty-third Psalm. "You know Him, Daddy. He's the Great Shepherd who saves to the 'uttermost.'"

I took his hand and he held on tight. "Do you remember? The 'uttermost.' Jesus saves to the 'uttermost.'"

I thought I saw recognition flash in his tired brown eyes. I know I saw peace.

After awhile he closed his eyes. I looked down, noticed that his bare feet stuck out of the covers. I touched them, took off my rust-colored sweater and wrapped it around them. I pulled the blanket close and tiptoed from the room.

Righteousness and Peace

Today as I read Hebrews 7 I see something besides the mysterious Melchizedek. I see Jesus. Just as His name means King of Righteousness and King of Peace for the Hebrew Christians so it is for Daddy.

For me.

To take the way of righteousness is to take the way God has provided through the death of His Son. It's coming to Him for forgiveness and being washed in His blood. It's believing that He will save to the "uttermost." It's experiencing His peace.

King of Righteousness, King of Peace, even the order whispers truth; righteousness always comes before peace. If there is no righteousness there is no peace. "For the kingdom of God is . . . righteousness and peace and joy in the Holy Spirit" (Rom. 14:17).

I reach for my journal, begin to write: *"The way of righteouness is simply accepting God's will. Even though He's my Savior and Lord I can't know lasting peace until every part of my being is touched with His Spirit.*

"The way of peace means knowing that God saves to the uttermost while I'm here on earth. But it means more—much more. Jesus is my guarantee that all God's promises will be fulfilled. His assurance is that His perfection will be my perfection, my body will be like His glorious body (Phil. 3:21). Even His ascension guarantees my entrance into heaven (John 14:3)."

Looking into the Face of Jesus

It's been over ten years now since Daddy went to heaven. Sometimes I picture Him and Jesus walking together beside the River of Life. Their arms are around one another's shoulders.

Daddy's steps are strong, his head high. I hear him laugh out loud, see the sparkle in his brown eyes.

Oh, Daddy, you knew, didn't you? When you were here on earth you looked into the Bible—God's own holy Word. When you did you saw the face of Jesus. You saw Him in all His love and righteousness and mercy.

You saw Him and knew you were seeing God. The God who saves to the "uttermost."

5

...

The New Covenant

Hebrews 8:1-13

❦ DAY 1 ❦

GOD SPEAKS

THE HEAVENLY SANCTUARY

1. Why are the things of earth more a reality to most people than the things in heaven?

   _____

   _____

   Read **Colossians 3:1-2.**
2. What are some things we can do to set our mind on things above?

_____

Read **Hebrews 8:1-2.**
3. According to these verses, what point has the writer already made?

_____

What names in these verses refer to Jesus?

_____

To God?

_____

What name is most significant to you right now? Put your thought into a statement or a prayer.

_____

_____

4. List several verses you've previously studied that reveal Jesus sitting at the right hand of God.

_____

Simon J. Kistemaker states that the verb *to sit down* is significant. He refers to the following quotation in his commentary on Hebrews.

Sitting was often a mark of honor, a king sat to receive his subjects, a court to give judgment, and a teacher to teach.[1]

5. Jesus serves as High Priest in the true tabernacle set up by the Lord. God Himself gave Moses a copy of this tabernacle (**Ex. 25:9, 40**) which was made on earth. But the true tabernacle is in

heaven. Where does Micah say the Lord God will come from when He comes to judge the earth (**Micah 1:2-3**)?

Where does the psalmist say He is (**Ps. 11:4**)?

_____

How does Isaiah see the Lord on His heavenly throne (**Isa. 6:1-4**)?

_____

_____

Both temple and throne are mentioned in **Revelation 16:17**. "Out of the temple came a loud voice from the throne, saying, 'It is done!'" (NIV). From this heavenly sanctuary flow blessings that are far greater than those that came from the Levitical sacrificial priesthood.

We serve a Superior Priest! a Mighty King! In what ways is Jesus even now serving you in heaven?

I LISTEN

Read **Revelation 3:20-21, 7:15-17**. What is Jesus promising to do for the one who comes to Him? For those who serve Him? Those who overcome? What is He saying to you right now?

I WORSHIP HIM

Give blessing and honor to Him who sits on the throne and to the Lamb. Worship Him who lives forever and ever. Amen.

❧ DAY 2 ❧

GOD SPEAKS

A BETTER SACRIFICE

Read **Hebrews 8:1-6.**
1. What is the best gift anyone ever gave you? What made it so significant? Tell about it.

_____

_____

2. The writer has already told us that high priests are appointed to
    offer sacrifices (See **Heb. 5:1**). Now in **8:3-4**, he contrasts the
    continual offerings of the high priest of gifts and sacrifices to the
    single offering Christ made on the cross. Read the following
    scriptures. Note one truth in each verse that is significant.

    Romans 6:23 _____

    Galatians 1:3-4 _____

    Ephesians 5:2 _____

    Ephesians 3:7 _____

    Hebrews 9:14 _____

    Hebres 10:12 _____

    Put a star by a verse you could share with someone in your
    family; an asterick, by one you could share with a friend; a cross,
    by one you could share with a co-worker.

3. **Hebrews 8:5** is a continuation of verse 4. The earthly priests
    served on earth, but Jesus served in heaven. The copy and shadow
    of the heavenly sacrifice is reflected on earth in the original
    sacrifices made by the priests.
        God Himself gave Moses divine instructions concerning how
    to build the tabernacle. Although its earthly form was a mere
    shadow of the heavenly original it did have form and substance.
        Jot down specific details in the instructions God gave Moses:

    Exodus 25:40 _____

    Exodus 26:30 _____

Exodus 27:8 _____

Numbers 8:4 _____

4. Read **Hebrews 8:6** in as many different translations as possible. For example *The Amplified Bible* says, "But as it now is, He [Christ] has acquired a [priestly] ministry which is as much superior and more excellent [than the old] as the covenant—the agreement—of which He is the Mediator [the Arbiter, Agent] is superior and more excellent; [because] it is enacted and rests upon more important [sublimer, higher and nobler] promises."

Why is the "But" that begins this verse significant?

_____

What do you think are the most important words in this verse?

_____

Choose one or two to look up in a dictionary. What additional insights do they give you into Christ's superior ministry?

_____

_____

I LISTEN

Describe Christ's more excellent ministry in your own life. How has He served you this week? This past month? This past year?

What would you like to see Him do for you or someone you love tomorrow? Next week? Talk to your Lord about your heart desires. He longs to reveal Himself to You as your Mediator. Your dearest friend.

I WORSHIP HIM

Praise Him for His excellent ministry in your life. He is worthy to be lifted high. To be exalted by the words of your lips.

❦ DAY 3 ❦

GOD SPEAKS

THE TWO COVENANTS

Read **Hebrews 8:7-13.**
1. Has anyone ever promised that if you did something, they would do something in response? How did it make you feel when they did what they said they would do? How did it make you feel when they failed to do what they said they would do?

_____

_____

In the Old Testament a covenant was an agreement entered into by two people. It was also used to describe the relationship between Israel and God. Before giving the law God graciously approached the people and invited them to enter into a special covenant with Him.

Read **Exodus 19:3-8.**
2. What did God ask Israel to do (v. 5)?

_____

If they did this, what did God promise would happen (v. 6)?

_____

What did the people commit to do (v. 8)?

_____

Read **Hebrews 8:7-8.**
3. How does the writer describe the first covenant?

_____

84

What is God promising for Israel and Judah?

_____

_____

Read **Hebrews 8:8-12.**

4. The writer to the Hebrews is quoting **Jeremiah 32:31-34.** We noted earlier in our study that his frequent quotations from lengthy passages in the Old Testament is characteristic of his writing. Usually he explains and applies them in the immediate context, but not this time. He's simply using them to prove that God Himself has already revealed that the old covenant would be replaced by the new.

    This new covenant is one of the great passages in the Bible. Read it over at least three times. Write down as many observations as you can. The following questions will help you get started. How many times do you read the words, "says the Lord" in this passage? Who is described as belonging to the house of Israel? What kind of knowledge is given to those who have God's laws in their heart?

_____

_____

_____

_____

_____

_____

_____

_____

_____

Getting to Know the Heart of God

5. God makes several unconditional promises to His people in these verses. Which one is most meaningful to you? Try to put your thoughts and feelings into words that you could share with a friend.

_____

_____

I LISTEN

There is something very precious about the phrase, "I will be their God, and they shall be My people" (8:10b). When people are saved because of Calvary, they are God's people in a way never before known. Personalize this sentence in your journal by changing the pronoun "their" to "your," "they" to "you" and "people" to "my special person."

I WORSHIP HIM

Thank Him for the new covenant. Ask Him to make it real to your heart, as you come before Him today.

❦ DAY 4 ❦

GOD SPEAKS

THE HEART OF GOD

Read **Hebrews 8:8-13.**

1. What would it mean to you to receive a gift that cost the giver something, was brand new, yet perfectly designed to meet your needs? Compare this gift with what you've already discovered about the new covenant.

_____

_____

_____

2. The new covenant reveals God's heart in a new and glorious way. Under the old covenant a person could keep his relationship with God only by obeying the law. But the new covenant is based entirely on God. What security does this truth give the child of God?

_____

William Barclay in *The Letter to the Hebrews* helps us understand the significance of the word *new.*

This covenant will not only be new; *it will be different in quality and in kind.* In Greek there are two words for *new. Neos* describes a thing as being new in point of time. It might be a precise copy of its predecessor, but since it has been made after the others, it is *neos. Kainos* means not only new in point of time, but new in point of quality. A thing which is simply a reproduction of what went before may be *neos* but it is not *kainos.* This covenant which Jesus introduces in *kainos* is not merely *neos;* it is different in quality from the old covenant.[2]

3. The new covenant is not only different, it is broader in scope than the old. Read the following verses and respond to the questions. **(v. 8)** With whom does God make this new covenant?

_____

In the days of Rehoboam the Israelite kingdom had been split into two nations; the ten tribes of Israel and the two belonging to Judah. The new covenant has power to unite that which has been divided. What hope does this give you?

_____

How has sin created division in your family?

_____

Your church?

_____

Your own life?

_____

What do you think God wants to do for you?

_____

b. **(v. 10)** The Jewish law caused a great separation between the Jews. Those who rigidly observed it looked down on those who didn't. Ordinary people just couldn't quite meet their standards or that of a holy God. But the new covenant promises, "I will _____;
and I will _____."

What hope does this two-fold promise give you?

_____

Where is it written?

_____

What does it mean to you to obey God, not out of fear, but out of love?

_____

_____

c. **(v. 11)** This verse doesn't mean we don't need teachers to explain God's Word. It does mean that God is promising that all men, woman and children can know the Lord. How can this truth give you confidence as you tell others about Jesus Christ and His sacrifice on Calvary?

_____

d. **(v. 12)** What confidence does this promise give to you? What does it mean for you to be forgiven of your sins?

_____

_____

e. **(v. 13)** What words does the writer use to describe the old covenant?

_____

What does it mean to you to know that the new covenant Jesus brought is not only new, it also cancels out the old?

_____

_____

I LISTEN

Describe the new covenant in words that make sense to you. How does it make you feel to realize your relationship to God is entirely dependent on God's love?

I WORSHIP HIM

Find the hymn, "Amazing Grace." Use the words as part of your worship today.

❦ DAY 5 ❦

GOD SPEAKS

THE NEW COVENANT AND A NEW PERSON

1. Charles Swindoll writes, "The bad news is that we've all made a mess of our lives and fallen short of the glory of God. The good news is that Jesus can take that spilled milk and turn it into ice cream."[3] Make your own word picture. Finish the sentence: The good news is that Jesus can _____

    _____

    _____

Read **Matthew 26:27-28** and **1 Corinthians 11:25.**

2. The writer of Hebrews isn't the only one to mention the new covenant. Jesus' own lips instituted it at the last supper. (Keep in mind that the same Greek word is translated as both "testament" and "covenant" in the New Testament.) How does your new understanding of this covenant heighten your appreciation of Jesus' sacrifice?

    _____

    _____

    Write down one new thought you can take with you the next time you participate in communion with your church family.

    _____

    _____

    _____

3. The message of the new covenant is also closely related to the message of **2 Corinthians 5:17**. The footnote in *The Holy Bible, The New King James Version, Prophecy Edition* says: "The new nature must be cultivated or nurtured by spiritual decisiveness to grow in Christ."[4] Just as the new covenant expresses the heart of God, so the exhortation to keep growing expresses His desire for each of His children to become mature.

Choose one or more of the following scripture passages to help you write a description of the new person Christ desires you to be. (Rom. 8:12-17, Gal. 5:22-26, Eph. 4:23–5:2) Or use your own scripture passage or selection of verses.

_____

_____

_____

I LISTEN

The Apostle Paul also writes about the new covenant. Compare Hebrews 8:10 with 2 Corinthians 3:2-6. How does it make you feel to know that God's laws are written in your mind and heart? That you are God's epistle known and read by all men?

The new covenant not only has power to change your life, it also has power to make you into a competent minister (2 Cor. 3:5-6). Ask the Lord what specific ministry He has for you to do today. What specific encouragement do these verses give you that will help you follow through?

_____

_____

I WORSHIP HIM

The new covenant has a glory that far exceeds the old covenant. Praise God for giving you this glorious ministry.

Challenge Activity: Contrast the Old Covenant with the New Covenant by creating an acrostic to describe each one.

O	N
L	E xpressive
D	W
C onvicting	C
O bsolete	O
V	V
E	E
N	N ecessary
A	A
N	N
T	T

WALKING ALONG TOGETHER

Mother hated to sew. She did it, though, because she loved me.

I remember the bright red skirt and vest she made when I was five. Everyone noticed me when I wore it. They patted the curl mother carefully brushed into place in the middle of my forehead and said, "My, my. It must be Little Red Riding Hood."

But the sewing project I most remember was the black and gray plaid coat. I can still see the gleam in mother's eye as she pulled the large coat out of a box of discards someone had given us.

"Eva Jane needs a nice winter coat," she said as she stroked the plaid. "I wonder. . . ." She turned to me. "Would you wear a coat made out of this fabric?"

Later I heard her talking to her friend, Ruth. "People do make them over you know. And Eva Jane likes it."

"But Jenny, I've heard it's more difficult to make one over than to actually start out new," Ruth said. "When you take it apart and cut it down smaller, it just gets harder and harder. And you don't have a pattern."

Mother sighed and then made her decision. "I'm going to do it. Eva Jane doesn't have a decent coat."

My New Coat

That evening after supper in the dim light of the kerosene lamp,

Mother began her project. She used a sharp razor to rip apart the seams. Then she laid the pieces on the floor, picked up her gleaming scissors and began to cut the pieces down to size.

The old treadle Singer machine whirred late into the night and gradually my coat emerged. It seemed like Mother spent hours adjusting a sleeve. Even the hem seemed to defy her as she pinned and adjusted, all on my own small wiggly unwilling self.

Looking back, I remember the process more than the product. I seem to recall Mother calling at me when I was outside, "Eva Jane, put on your coat." But I didn't want to—the collar made my neck itch and the lining twisted around inside and made my arms feel funny. Sometimes I felt guilty. Mother had worked so hard to make it and though I'd agreed to wear it, I soon failed to do so.

Sometimes I wonder what became of that plaid coat. Did it vanish into the ragbag? End up in someone else's box of discards?

The Old Covenant

I thought about my old coat today when I read about the old covenant God had made with Israel. Was it words like *obsolete, growing old, ready to vanish away* that made me remember? Or the verse about no place would have been sought for a second if the first had been without a fault?

I only knew that my heart was ready for the new covenant—I knew what it was like to have to make do with something that was less than perfect. As I read I reveled over God's description of that covenant— His law written in my mind, my heart, my innermost being. His promise that He would be my God and I would be His special woman. His promise that I would know Him—as one friend knows another.

Hebrews 8:12 sparkles at me. "For I will be merciful to their unrighteousness, and their sins and their lawless deeds I will remember no more."

I reach for my journal, write: *"I know what sin and unrighteousness can do. I know the power they have to shipwreck a life—even my own and I'm so aware of my own need for cleansing.*

"Lord God, there's a big blob of unforgiveness deep inside me. I'll be doing just fine and then—all of a sudden, up it comes—a great black wave of resentment and bitterness.

"Be gracious to me, O God, according to Thy lovingkindness; according to the greatness of Thy compassion blot out my transgressions. Wash me thoroughly from my iniquity, and cleanse me from my

sin (Ps. 51:1-2 NASB).

Another verse comes from my Lord. "I, even I, am he who blots out your transgressions, for my own sake, and remembers your sins no more" (Isa. 43:25 NIV).

With that reassurance comes a glory thought. Because I've been forgiven I can forgive others. It's a part of the new covenant.

"Therefore, as God's chosen people, holy and dearly beloved, clothe yourselves with compassion, kindness, humility, gentleness and patience. Bear with each other and forgive whatever grievances you may have against one another. Forgive as the Lord forgave you. And over all these virtues put on love, which binds them all together in perfect unity" (Col. 3:12-14 NIV).

The glory of forgiveness wraps itself around my spirit. Because I'm unconditionally forgiven I can forgive others. When we are dressed in His forgiveness, His love is a crimson sash that binds us all together.

The Gold Coat

Suddenly I remember another coat—not the black and gray plaid of my childhood—a brand new coat, my very first—and I'm just sixteen. The coat is soft gold and the lines flow with my figure. The sleeves are silken and roomy, and when I slip my arms into it I feel like a queen. The gold accentuates the lights in my hair. I tie the sash around my waist and I'm off.

The memory makes me smile. As lovely as my gold coat was the garment of forgiveness my Savior wove for me on the cross far surpasses it. I'm dressed in His righteousness, adorned in His grace.

The words of my favorite psalm sing through my soul.

"The king's daughter is all glorious within; her clothing is of wrought gold. She shall be brought unto the king in raiment of needlework; the virgins, her companions, who follow her, shall be brought unto you.

"With gladness and rejoicing shall they be brought; they shall enter into the king's palace" (Ps. 45:13-15).

"King of righteousness, I love you."

6

...

Worshiping
in the Tabernacle

Hebrews 9:1-15

❦   **DAY 1**   ❦

GOD SPEAKS

THE TABERNACLE

Read **Hebrews 9:1-6.**

1. Describe a place that drew you to worship God. Was it inside a
    church? a garden? What externals were there that drew your heart
    in God's direction?

    _____

    _____

Getting to Know the Heart of God

2. The tabernacle the writer to the Hebrews called attention to in **9:1-6** contained a variety of furnishings arranged in a way that stimulated the people's worship of God. List the furnishings:

_____

_____

Observe significant details:

_____

_____

3. Why do you think the writer omitted important details about the tabernacle's beauty (**v. 5**)?

_____

The main description of the tabernacle in the wilderness is in **Exodus 25-31** and **35-40**. Read what you can. Note specific details about the articles mentioned in **Hebrews 9:1**—the lampstand (Ex. 25:31-40), the table and showbread (Ex. 25:23-30), the altar of incense (Ex. 30:1-10) and the ark of the covenant in the Holy place (Ex. 25:10-22).

_____

_____

_____

_____

4. According to **Exodus 25:8**, what was God's purpose for the first tabernacle?

_____

The following quotation by William Barclay in the *Letter to the Hebrews* gives additional insights:

> The writer to the Hebrews had just been thinking of Jesus as the one who leads us into reality. He has been using the idea that in this world we have only pale copies of what is truly real. The worship that men can offer is only a ghostlike shadow of the real worship which Jesus, the real High Priest, alone can offer. But even as he thinks of that his mind goes back to the Tabernacle (the Tabernacle, remember, not the Temple). Lovingly he remembers its beauty; lovingly he lingers on its priceless possessions. And the thought in his mind is this—if earthly worship was as beautiful as this, what must the true worship be like? If all the loveliness of the Tabernacle was only a shadow of reality, how surpassingly lovely the reality must be.[1]

I LISTEN

The Holy of Holies had a beauty that almost defies description. Each intricate detail shouts, "glory!"—but none quite as loudly as the "Cherubim of glory." This expression is an obvious reference to the glory of our Lord Jesus Christ. Read **1 Timothy 6:15-16**. How has the one who dwells in unapproachable light revealed Himself to you today?

I WORSHIP HIM

Which of Jesus' titles in 1 Timothy 6:15-16 is most meaningful to you? Call Him by that title as you praise Him.

❧ DAY 2 ❧

GOD SPEAKS

GLIMPSES OF HIS GLORY

Read **Hebrews 9:1-6.**
1. God often uses symbolism to communicate heavenly truth to His people. What symbol or symbols are most significant to you?

The writer of Hebrews appears to be so eager to show his readers that the insufficiency of gifts and sacrifices were not able to "perfect . . . the conscience" of the Israelite worshipers that he's almost abrupt in his departure from the tabernacle furniture. He wants to move on to the wonder of Christ's sacrifice for sin!

But scholars have seen glimpses of Jesus' glory in these furnishings. Let's linger in the tabernacle.

2. Compare the following scriptures about Jesus Christ to the various furnishings mentioned in these verses. Write a truth you discover about Jesus beneath each one. (The last two are done for you).
    a. The lampstand (John 1:4, 9; 8:12; 9:5)

    b. The table of showbread (John 6:35, 48-51; 1 Pet. 2:9; Rev. 2:6)

    c. The Ark of the Covenant
        C.I. Scofield in the *The New Scofield Reference Bible* notes that the aracia wood and gold are types of Christ. "Acacia wood, a desert growth, is a fitting symbol of Christ in His humanity as 'a root out of a dry ground' (Isa. 53:2). The covering, gold, typifying Deity in manifestation, speaks of His divine glory."[2]
        The pot of manna and the showbread allude to Jesus as the Bread of Life (John 6:48-51, 57, 58); Aaron's rod, to His resurrection (John 11:25): the tablets of stone, to God's laws hidden in the heart (Heb. 8:10). The mercy seat of gold overshadowed by the wings of the cherubim speak of His glory and His mercy for the sinner. To the sinning Israelites the mercy seat was a throne of grace, sprinkled with the blood of sacrifice.

    d. The altar of incense reminds us that Jesus is our Mediator and

Intercessor at the throne of heaven—through Him our prayers and praises ascend to God (Heb. 7:25).

3. Complete the following sentences:
Because Jesus is the Light of the word I can _____

_____

Because Jesus is the Bread of Life I can _____

_____

Because Jesus is the Resurrection and the Life I can _____

_____

Because His law is written in my heart I can _____

_____

Because Jesus is my Mediator and His throne is the throne of grace I can _____

_____

I LISTEN

The prayers of the saints are also referred to as incense (Rev. 5:8, 8:3-4). How does it make you feel to realize that your prayers are even now before God's throne? Draw a picture of incense ascending heavenward. Write in some of your prayers.

I WORSHIP HIM

Thank God for sending His Son to be your Mediator who is even now interceding for you at the Father's right hand at the throne in heaven.

❧ DAY 3 ❧

GOD SPEAKS

ENTERING THE HOLY PLACE

Read **Hebrews 9:6-11.**
1. Describe an act of worship you take part in during a service at
    your church? Why is it significant?

_____

_____

_____

In verse 6 the writer of Hebrews refers to the ceremonies the
priests performed in the tabernacle as a part of their worship.
Although the writer and his readers were familiar with these
ordinances, most believers today aren't.

In order to understand chapters 9 and 10 we need to go back to
Leviticus 16. This chapter gives a detailed description of the
priest's entry into the Holiest of All on the Day of Atonement.

Read **Leviticus 16.**
2. What specific instructions did God give Moses to give to Aaron,
    the high priest?

_____

Describe his dress:

_____

Identify the sacrifices that Aaron was to present before the Lord.

_____

Why was Aaron required to make two offerings for sin?

_____

3. *Atonement* is an important word in this chapter. Look up *atone-ment* in your concordance. How many times is it used in the Old Testament?

   Look it up in the dictionary. Compare it with what you are learning in this chapter and write a definition.

_____

What was the significance of the many washings (vv. **4, 24-28, 30**)?

_____

Why is **Leviticus 16:33** a good summary verse for the High Priest's ministry on that great day, the Day of Atonement?

_____

4. The Day of Atonement, this great and holy day which was so important to the Israelites, is in the writer's mind as he writes. What two words does he use to bring his discussion back to Jesus (**Heb. 9:11**)?

_____

Why are they significant?

_____

I LISTEN

"But Christ. . . ." These two words are powerful. What situation or circumstances do you face today that needs this reminder—"But Christ. . . ."? Describe it in your journal. But don't stop there. Allow Jesus to enter into it with you by writing "But Christ. . . ." and continue writing. Ask God to give you insights into how Jesus wants to impact your problem/need/attitude by His Spirit.

Getting to Know the Heart of God

I WORSHIP HIM

When the high priest entered the Holy of Holies, he wore a breast-plate of twelve stones with the names of each of the twelve tribes inscribed thereon. He was literally bearing the names of those he loved upon his shoulders. Jesus does that, too. Your name is inscribed on His heart. Praise Him now for interceding for you by name at the throne of God.

❧ DAY 4 ❧

GOD SPEAKS

THE BEAUTY OF THE BLOOD

Read **Hebrews 9:11-14.**

"You Christians worship a gory God. All your talk about Jesus' blood—it sickens me." These words were spoken by a woman who wanted nothing to do with sin or sacrifice. A moral and self-made woman, she despised any reference to "the blood of the Lamb."

1. How would you explain Christ's shed blood to someone who knew nothing about the significance of sacrifice?

    _____

    _____

2. **Hebrews 9:11-14** is significant. Prayerfully read and reread, then write down as many observations as you can about the passage. Look for names used for God, repeated words, important words you may not yet understand.

    _____

    _____

    _____

3. Those two important questions you need to ask in order to understand a scripture passage will help you unlock the richness of these verses. Condense your thoughts into one or two sentences for each question.

    What is the author saying?

    _____

    What is he saying about it?

    _____

4. What does God want to do for every believer (**v. 14**)?

    _____

    As a result, what will we be able to do?

    _____

    Respond to this sentence: Worship begins at the altar of sacrifice. How have you discovered this to be true in your life?

    _____

    _____

I LISTEN

Not only did Jesus pay the sacrifice of blood for your sins, He made it possible for you to have victory. What does God want to purge from your life in order that you may serve Him better?

I WORSHIP HIM

Find a chorus or hymn that proclaims the blood of Jesus. Make the words your own praise song as you worship.

❦ DAY 5 ❦

GOD SPEAKS

JESUS IN THE TABERNACLE

Read Hebrews 9:11-14.

1. A four-year-old boy told his mother, "Jesus is God dressed up." What deep truth about Jesus has this small child begun to understood?

_____

_____

This world is a world of shadows and imperfect copies—the truth Jesus brings is the only true reality—the reality of eternity. God designed worship to bring men and women into contact with these eternal realites. His purpose for the tabernacle and its worship were to bring us into His presence. But these were only shadows of the real thing.

The new tabernacle in verse 11 is the body of Jesus. In Him God entered our world in human form. When we see Jesus we see God (John 14:9).

2. What do you discover about the new and greater tabernacle in the verses that follow (**Heb. 9:12-14**)?

a. _____

b. _____

c. _____

d. _____

3. Christ's death not only frees a woman from the power of sin, it also frees her to serve Him in a new and living way. Look up the

words *servant* and/or *serve* in a concordance. Use several of these references to write a definition of a servant who pleases God.

_____

_____

Challenge activity: Underline the recurring "much more" phrases in Romans 5:6-21. Compare these verses to Hebrews 9:11-14. What similar theme binds the two passages together? What additional insights do the verses in Romans give you about the grace of God? God's gift of salvation? What verse could you use to show someone the love of Christ?

I LISTEN
Read **Hebrews 13:12**. Jesus suffered and died on the cross outside Jerusalem. He carried the reproach of our sin outside the city. Use one of the passages on the crucifixion to contemplate what He did for you. Seek to understand the reality of His sacrifice.

I WORSHIP HIM
The cross shows us a God who expresses His love in the outstretched arms of Jesus. Bow before Him. Acknowledge the greatness of His love.

WALKING ALONG TOGETHER
More than anything I wanted a home and children when I grew up. Maybe that was why I decided to build a playhouse out in the old sheep pasture.

We called that particular part of the property, "The Point" because it was shaped like a piece of pie and jutted off our 30-acre farm like a pointing finger. It was a place of jack fern and hazelnut bushes with a few spindly oaks. The sheep had woven tiny trails through the fern, and occasional open space let sunshine in.

Building a Playhouse
After Daddy moved the sheep to another pasture, I took over "The Point." It was here I built my house.

I chose a grassy clearing surrounded by tall fern and spindly oaks for a living room. A clump of hazelnut bushes became a closet. I stomped down ferns to make room for a kitchen and brought old red bricks from home to build a cookstove. Galvanized jar lids Mother used for canning became cooking pans; flat glass ones were plates. Sticks broken into appropriate lengths served as utensils. My kitchen was complete.

After that I made two bedrooms. Piles of carefully selected fern fronds were arranged into beds for me and my children. I chose another clump of hazelnut for a closet and our house was ready.

Another trip home and Mary Ann and my Raggedy Ann doll joined me in my new house. With them came invisible twin baby girls I envisioned as my own.

Another House

I smile when I think back to my house on "The Point." In a way it was a kind of forerunner for the real house my husband Bud and I built on that same piece of property years later.

My father gave us "The Point" and our house went up board by board. Today green lawns grace the place where jack fern and hazelnuts once grew. The tiny oak trees became stately giants who now welcome our friends beside our front door. They spread their protective arms over our house and yard and provide shade for picnics and romps with the grandchildren.

In a way my playhouse was a shadow—a phantom—a silhouette of the real home I would one day enjoy with my husband Bud. Could it be that Mary Ann and Raggedy Ann were but pale copies of the six children I would one day have? That those imaginary twin girls were but shadows of the two-year-old twin granddaughters who now grace my daughter's home?

I can only wonder.

The Place of His Presence

Shadows. Phantoms. Silhouettes. We call it the real world, but is it? No, in this world we walk in shadows. Jesus is the only one who can lead us into reality—the unseen place where God's glory dwells.

Today as I study Hebrews 9, I can know that the tabernacle in the wilderness was a mere shadow of Jesus Christ and His sacrifice for my sins. His body broken for me is the only way I have been granted access into the presence of God. It's Jesus who leads me there.

Suddenly I'm remembering a picture the Holy Spirit gave me—Jesus Christ bending low over me. A song—He's singing to me His love.

"Do not fear, O [Eva]; do not let your hands hang limp. The LORD your God is with you, he is mighty to save. He will take great delight in you, he will quiet you with his love, he will rejoice over you with singing" (Zeph. 3:16-17 NIV).

My Lord Jesus Christ, rejoicing over me with song . . . a new song . . . the song of the new covenant.

I open my Bible. I have to hear the new song as it's sung in the heavenly realm. I have to.

A New Song

I find the song I'm searching for in Revelation.

"And I looked, and behold, in the midst of the throne and of the four living creatures, and in the midst of the elders, stood a Lamb as though it had been slain, having seven horns and seven eyes, which are the seven Spirits of God sent out into all the earth.

"Then He came and took the scroll out of the right hand of Him who sat on the throne. Now when He had taken the scroll, the four living creatures and the twenty-four elders fell down before the Lamb, each having a harp, and golden bowls full of incense, which are the prayers of the saints.

"And they sang a new song, saying:
'You are worthy to take the scroll,
And to open its seals;
For You were slain,
And have redeemed us to God by Your blood
Out of every tribe and tongue and people and nation,
And have made us kings and priests to our God;
And we shall reign on the earth.'

"Then I looked, and I heard the voice of many angels around the throne, the living creatures, and the elders; and the number of them was ten thousand times ten thousand, and thousands of thousands, saying with a loud voice:
"'Worthy is the Lamb who was slain
To receive power and riches and wisdom,
And strength and honor and glory and blessing!'

"And every creature which is in heaven and on the earth and under the earth and such as are in the sea, and all that are in them, I heard saying:

"'Blessing and honor and glory and power

Be to Him who sits on the throne,

And to the Lamb, forever and ever!'

"Then the four living creatures said, 'Amen!' And the twenty-four elders fell down and worshiped Him who lives forever and ever" (Rev. 5:6-14).

Reflections of His Glory

Just as the earthly temple was only a pale copy of the heavenly temple, so earthly worship is only a remote reflection of real worship, the worship of heaven.

I open my notebook, write five words—*"Jesus is reality. Amen. Amen."*

I worship in His presence.

7
...

Behold the Lamb!

Hebrews 9:15–10:18

❦ DAY 1 ❦

GOD SPEAKS

THE BLOOD THAT CLEANSES

Read **Hebrews 9:15-28.**
1.   Have you or someone you know ever been mentioned in someone's
     will? What did you or they receive as an inheritance?

     _____

     How did it make you feel to know that in order to receive that
     inheritance someone had to die?

_____

_____

2.   The opening phrase in the verse that begins today's study says,
     "And for this reason" is there for a reason. Look at the preceding
     context. Pay particular attention to the contrast between the sacri-
     fices of the old covenant and the new covenant in verses 13 and
     14. Summarize in your own words the writer's reason as to how
     and why Christ is the mediator of a new covenant.

_____

_____

3.   The emphasis of Hebrews **9:15-28** is blood. How many times
     does the writer use this word?

_____

     Write down as many additional words as you can that relate to
     blood and cleansing.

_____

_____

     Another important word in this passage is *testament. The Ampli-
     fied Bible* helps us understand (vv. 16-18):

     For where there is a {last} will *and* testament involved, the
     death of the one who made it must be established. For a will
     and testament is valid and takes effect only at death, since it
     has no force *or* legal power as long as the one who made it is
     alive. So even the (old) first covenant [God's will] was not
     inaugurated *and* ratified *and* put in force without the shed-
     ding of blood.

110

Under God's terms, this testament (will) was signed, sealed and delivered in blood. The old covenant was also instituted by the shedding of blood.

4. Read **Exodus 24:1-8**.
   Compare **verse 8** with **Hebrews 9:20**. What do you observe?

   _____

5. How does Jesus' blood relate to forgiveness (**Heb. 9:22** and **Mark 14:24**)?

   _____

   What more do you discover about blood and forgiveness from **Leviticus 17:11**?

   _____

I LISTEN

Forgiveness always costs somebody something. Respond to the following quotation from William Barclay in the *Letter to the Hebrews* in your journal.

> God alone can pay the terrible price that is necessary before men can be forgiven. Forgiveness is never a case of saying: "It's all right; it doesn't matter." It is the most costly thing in the world. Without the shedding of heart's blood there can be no forgiveness of sins. Nothing brings a man to his senses with such arresting violence as to see the effect of his sin on someone who loves him in this world or on the God who loves him forever and to say to himself: "It cost *that* to forgive my sin." Where there is forgiveness someone must be crucified.[1]

I WORSHIP HIM

Hebrews 9 and 10 reveal the heart of God in a unique and beautiful way. It is here that we see Jesus, the Shepherd who became the Lamb, as the High Priest who became the Sacrifice. Like John the Baptist,

111

the writer of Hebrews points to Jesus and proclaims, "Behold! The Lamb of God who takes away the sin of the world!" (John 1:29b)

Worship the Lamb!

❦ DAY 2 ❦

GOD SPEAKS

THEREFORE . . .

Read **Hebrews 9:23-28.**

The first word in verse 23 is "therefore." So placed, it is a beautiful word—it brings us into this passage so that we can know we are personally involved. Salvation is real! Think about it for a moment.

1. What does your salvation mean to you?

   _____

   _____

2. Look back over the observations you made yesterday concerning the blood. Read verses 23-28 again. How does blood relate to your salvation?

   _____

   _____

3. There are two contrasts in verses 24-26:
   a. Christ didn't enter a holy place on earth; he entered heaven itself.
   b. _____

   What does this mean to you?

   _____

_____

4. Chapter 9 concludes with a warning and a promise. What is the warning in verse 27?

_____

An understanding of the word *judgement* will help you better appreciate verse 28. Look it up in a dictionary. Write down the definition that refers to the use of the word as it is used in this verse.

_____

Read **Hebrews 6:2 and 9:27.**
5. What more do you discover about God's judgment?

_____

Use your concordance to find at least five other references that refer to the judgment of those who refuse to be cleansed by Jesus' blood. Write them down.

_____

_____

6. What action do these verses inspire you to take?

_____

Read **Hebrews 9:28.**
7. What encouragement is there for you here?

_____

The good news of Hebrews 9 is that we escape eternal judgment when our hearts are washed in the blood of the Lamb. How does this truth make you feel?

113

I LISTEN

Just as the people expectantly waited for the high priest to come out of the Holy of Holies on the Day of Atonement, so should we expectantly wait for Jesus Christ to appear the second time. What about you? Are you eagerly waiting to meet Him? Do you long to see His eyes? Feel His arms around you?

I WORSHIP HIM

This chapter closes with a glorious hope. Christ is coming again! He came the first time to die for our sins. He comes the second time to bring us salvation in all its fullness. Therefore . . . praise Him.

❦ DAY 3 ❦

GOD SPEAKS

THE ONLY TRUE SACRIFICE

Read **Hebrews 10:1-4.**

1. Has anyone ever told you not to do something and immediately you wanted to do it? Tell about it.

   _____

   _____

2. Worship under the law was specific and detailed—what the priests wore, how the animals were sacrificed and what days were to be observed. How is the law referred to in verse 1?

   _____

   The phrase "the very image of the things" suggests a dim outline of the real thing. Although the law and the sacrifices were a matter of life or death, they had their limitations. What were

114

some of the things they could not do?

a. **(v. 1)** _____

b. **(v. 2)** _____

c. **(v. 4)** _____

3. The law with its regulations of worship can't make anyone perfect or clean, nor permanently remove sin. But according to verse 3 it does do one thing. What is it?

_____

4. Read **Romans 3:19-23.**
   The law doesn't erase sin, it only underlines it. Just as a speed limit sign makes us feel guilty when we drive past the limit, so the Law reminded the Israelites of their sins. Of what essential truth in verse 23 does God remind us today?

_____

I LISTEN

The Greek word for *image* means a complete or detailed representation. A writer explaining the same concept to us today would probably use the word, *photograph.*

Explore these questions in your journal: How does an animal sacrifice picture Jesus' sacrifice on the cross for your sin? How does the Lamb of God, the perfect sacrifice, make this incomplete picture perfect?

Design a symbol that represents what you're discovering about the heart of God as expressed in Jesus' sacrifice for your sin will help you clarify truth.

I WORSHIP HIM

Hebrews 10:4 makes a strong statement concerning the ineffectiveness of animal sacrifices. This statement beautifully transitioned us to Jesus who is the only perfect sacrifice (v. 5). Worship God now by thanking Him for Jesus' body, prepared as a sacrifice, to meet the needs of a world dying in sin.

❦ DAY 4 ❦

GOD SPEAKS

A FOREVER SACRIFICE

Charles Swindoll says, "The Lord Jesus Christ did not come with a lamb in his arms to offer to God. Instead, He came as the Lamb of God and voluntarily gave Himself up as the sacrifice."[2]

1. How does your heart respond to this word picture?

   _____

Read Hebrews 10:5-14.
2. Jesus is again introduced into the context of law and sacrifice by the word "therefore." The verses (Heb. 10:5-7) the writer quotes from Psalm 40:6-8 show the contrast between the animal sacrifices and Christ.

   The animals that were sacrificed for the sins of the people had no will of their own. How is this different from Christ's sacrifice?

   _____

   What do these verses show you about the heart of God?

   _____

3. Two significant phrases from verse 7 are put together in verse 9. Compare **Hebrews 10:9** with **Matthew 26:39-42**. What did it mean for Jesus to do the will of His Father?

   _____

Read Hebrews 10:9-10 again.
4. Jesus set aside the _____(first) in order to establish _____ (the second) when He offered His body "once for all." His will

116

submitted to His Father resulted in our _____.

The word *sanctified* means "to be set aside for an intended use." What does it mean to you to realize that God has set you aside for His own special purpose?

_____

_____

What is that purpose?

_____

5. Another contrast is made in **vv. 11-14**. Complete the following: The priest stands _____ (v. 11). But this Man (Jesus), after He had offered_____ sat down at the right hand of God (v. 12).

   Many sacrifices—one sacrifice, but the writer uses still another contrast. Underline the two verbs that show the posture of the priests and Jesus.

   Jesus' sitting down at the right hand of God speak of a finished work. It reminds us of His last words on the cross. What were they (**John 19:30**)?

_____

How is Jesus' finished work different from our so called finished tasks?

_____

_____

I LISTEN

The writer of Hebrews uses the word *sanctified* again in verse 14. This time he's using it in the present tense—"those who *are being* sanctified." (Verse 10 refers to our having *been* sanctified by Jesus' obedience to God's will, even unto the death of the cross.)

Look up *sanctify* in a dictionary. As you write down the definition,

117

ask the Holy Spirit to reveal how you can be made holy on a daily basis (1 Pet. 1:13-16)?

I WORSHIP HIM

No other sacrifice in the world has power to do for you what Jesus' sacrifice did. Praise Him for His once for all offering—His forever offering that forever satisfied the heart of God.

❦ DAY 5 ❦

GOD SPEAKS

THE BENEFITS OF GRACE

1. What are some of the things you've been told you couldn't do if you were to keep in God's favor?

   _____

   _____

   What are some of the things you've been told you must do in order to win His approval?

   _____

   _____

Read **Hebrews 10:15-18**.
2. God doesn't want us to live our lives chained by check lists of do's and don'ts. He wants us to be free, to live free. In these few verses the writer concludes this part of his teaching on the new covenant. Who is it that bears witness of this new life of freedom?

   _____

3. Once again the writer refers to the promise of the new covenant

(Jer. 31:33-34) quoted in Hebrews 8. Before he does, however, he reminds us again who the real Author of scripture is. What is the Holy Spirit saying in these verses?

_____

_____

Carefully compare **Hebrews 10:16-17** with **Jeremiah 31:31-34.**
What is new in Jeremiah's prophecy that is now being quoted by the writer in Hebrews? Although Old Testament believers had experienced God's forgiving grace (see **Psalm 32:5; 103:12**), God is now telling His people in Hebrews 10:17 that He has forgiven their sins through Christ's sacrifice and will never recall them.

4. Allow your heart to respond to the forgetfulness of God as you personalize **Hebrews 10:17** into your own words.

_____

5. Look up _remission_ in the dictionary. How does its definition heighten your understanding of forgiveness (**Heb. 10:18**)?

_____

_____

This verse sums up a beautiful truth. What is it?

_____

_____

Challenge Activity: God's Word has always cried out that the only sacrifice God wanted was the obedience of His people. Read these scriptures: **1 Samuel 15:22; Psalm 50:14, 51:16-17; Hosea 6:6; Isaiah 1:11-20; Micah 6:6-8.** What more do they tell you about the heart of God?

Getting to Know the Heart of God

I LISTEN

God's Spirit within you enables you to live life freely and fruitfully under the umbrella of His grace. Read **Galatians 5:16-23**. Think of God's grace becoming evident in your life through the spiritual fruit listed in **v. 22-23**. How are these different from the things you listed on your lists of don'ts and do's in question 1?

Which of these fruits do you most long to experience in your life this week? Write a prayer that expresses the desire of your heart. You might even want to write a description of the fruit of your choice. Or draw a picture of it. Be creative!

I WORSHIP HIM

The new covenant reminds us: No more sacrifices! No more offerings! No more blood! Put your praise into a song!

WALKING ALONG TOGETHER

My mother loved her mother dearly. But while Grandma was on earth a certain pain was present, too. She was a Roman Catholic who deeply grieved that three of her daughters had chosen to become Protestants. My mother was one of them.

One of my mother's greatest concerns was that Grandma might not be saved. Sometimes we prayed out loud for her.

I was warming myself in front of the wood stove the day Mother came in with Grandma's letter in her hand. I looked up, surprised at the emotion I read on her face.

"Listen to Grandma's letter, Eva Jane," she exclaimed. "Oh, listen."

She unfolded the letter and began to read. When she came to the words she so wanted me to hear, she choked up. "She says, 'Oh, Jenny, the most important thing in the world is that Jesus died for our sins. Nothing is more important than the blood of Jesus Christ. It's something we must never forget.'"

Now that I've grown I've often thought of Grandma's letter. She died when I was twelve but I have the assurance that we'll spend eternity together.

Grandma believed in the precious blood of the Lamb.

A River of Blood

Today I read Hebrews 9 and 10 and remembered Grandma's letter.

The glory of the tabernacle, the glory of the covenant, the glory of my God.

What must it have been like for the Hebrew readers to have heard these chapters for the very first time? They knew firsthand the glory of the temple. They also knew the gory—the bleat of a sheep at the touch of the knife, the terror in its eyes as it faced death. The blood— pouring from the altar—an ever increasing stream that flowed on and on and on. . . . One generation of priests succeeding another, another helpless lamb born to die. . . . Another sin—another sacrifice. . . .

A virtual river of blood. An ineffectual one at that. There is no salvation apart from trusting in the blood of the Lamb.

Sacrifice . . . Cleansing . . . Redemption

I lean back in my chair. Sacrifice . . . redemption . . . the Mediator of a new covenant . . . without the shedding of blood there is no forgiveness.

A knock and I jump to my feet. My friend Sylvia stands at the door smiling at me. She gestures at my Bible and notebook as she sits down.

"Where are you today in your study, Eva?" she asks.

"Hebrews 9 and 10. The sprinkled blood. Christ the Mediator of a new covenant. Sylvia, the presence of the Living God is a very real thing."

She looks at me. "It shows. Even your face sort of glows."

I smile. "All I was doing was writing down observations on the two chapters. I feel like I've been in the Holy of Holies."

I continue. "There's something very wonderful about the blood of our Lord. I'm feeling it more and more. To think that our Lord had to shed His in order that we, sinful men and woman, can come into the presence of God, almost overwhelms me."

Sylvia nods. "Forgiveness is a costly thing. It comes directly from God."

A Story of Forgiveness

In a Scottish village there lived a doctor who was noted for both his professional skill and his devotion to Christ. After his death his books were examined. "Forgiven . . . too poor to pay" had been written in red across several of his entries."

Unfortunately his wife felt differently. She filed a suit before a court insisting that all debts be paid—no exceptions.

Getting to Know the Heart of God

When the case was heard, the judge asked, "Is this your husband's handwriting in red?"

She replied that it was.

"Then," said the judge, "not a tribunal in the land can obtain the money from those whom he has forgiven."

Redemption's Song

Sylvia looks at me. "We have that assurance, don't we, Eva? Christ's death satisfied God's demand that our sin debt be paid.

"Just before His death, Jesus said 'Tetelastai,' which means, 'paid in full.' Our sins have been forgiven because Jesus paid in full for them. His death secured our redemption, inheritance, forgiveness. He is our Redeemer in the fullest sense of the word."

After Sylvia leaves, I open my journal. I want to write a song to my Redeemer. I want to call it Redemption's Song.

But no music comes.

Instead I write: *"When the writer of Hebrews wanted to communicate what Christ did on the cross he used a word familiar to the ancient readers—redemption.*

"The Bible teaches that we all were slaves of the enemies of God— sin and Satan. Jesus Christ Himself entered the slave market to pay the purchase price of all persons triumphantly displayed by Satan who holds them captive with chains of sin too strong for any man or woman or child to break free.

"Jesus paid the price demanded for their freedom. Call it ransom, call it the purchase price. It is the blood of the Lamb.

"This is the good news that the book of Hebrews proclaims. None of us needs to be dominated by sin. Jesus died on the cross to purchase our redemption.

"One sacrifice once for all—powerful enough to make even His enemies bow before Him. One sacrifice once for all—finished for all eternity. One sacrifice once for all—to satisfy forever the heart of God.

I stop. There's music in the lines I've just written. *"One sacrifice once for all!"* It is redemption's song! The song of the new covenant. The song my grandmother sang.

It is my song, too. *"One sacrifice once for all—to satisfy forever the heart of God."*

"Lamb of God, I love You."

122

8

...

Therefore Remember. . . .

Hebrews 10:19-39

❦ **DAY 1** ❦

GOD SPEAKS

AN INVITATION TO ENTER

Read **Hebrews 10:19-22.**
1.   Where is the place you most like to go when you meet with God?

_____

2.   Chapter 9 began in a place, the tabernacle, then moved into the ministry performed there by the high priest on the Day of Atonement. The writer's comparison of that priestly ministry to Christ's ministry and His death on the cross is inlaid over it—the new

covenant, the blood of the Lamb—a mosaic of forgiveness and glory. Emblazoned over all is a simple invitation, "Come into My presence. Let the blood of the covenant cleanse your conscience that you might serve the living God."

Chapter 10 continues this mosaic of glory by taking us into the Holy of Holies—the holiest place that has ever been on earth. Summarize what you discovered there last week in the first 18 verses.

_____

_____

3. Read **Hebrews 10:19-22** in several translations if you have access to them. The NIV translation says:

> Therefore brothers, since we have confidence to enter the Most Holy Place by the blood of Jesus, by a new and living way opened for us through the curtain, that is, his body, and since we have a great priest over the house of God, let us draw near to God with a sincere heart in full assurance of faith, having our hearts sprinkled to cleanse us from a guilty conscience and having our bodies washed with pure water.

Not only do these verses transition from the doctrinal teaching just given on Christ's high priestly ministry, they set the stage for the three important commands that follow. Write down as many observations as you can from this passage (Heb. 10:19-22).

_____

_____

_____

4. A thick tapestried veil (curtain) separated the Holy of Holies from the rest of the temple. When Jesus died (Matt. 27:51) this veil that had kept people away for centuries was torn from top to bottom.

Now the writer of Hebrews invites us to enter the Holy Place deep within our souls—the inward place where God dwells when we receive Him as our Savior. He even encourages us to enter with an attitude of _____.

How is the way into the Holy Place described in **v. 20**?

_____

Simon J. Kistemaker in his commentary of Hebrews explains "the way" this way:

> The term way is described as "new and living." Unfortunately the translation of "new" is incomplete, for the Greek word actually means "just slaughtered." It is a term relating to religious sacrifices. The adjective living signifies that the way Christ has opened up for us is not a road without an exit: a dead-end street. Rather, this road leads us to salvation, into the very presence of God.
>
> Christ has dedicated the way by opening the curtain, "that is, his body." At his death the curtain to the Most Holy Place had to be torn from top to bottom. Likewise the body of Jesus had to be broken, and his blood had to be shed to open for us the way to God. By his sacrifice on the cross, Christ has removed the veil between God and his people.[1]

5. Some commentators interpret *house* to mean heaven, others, the church (**v. 21**). But could it be our bodies?
   Examine the following scriptures. What do you think?

   Hebrews 3:6 _____

   1 Corinthians 6:19 _____

   2 Corinthians 6:16 _____

6. **Hebrews 4:16** and **Hebrews 10:22** are parallel passages. Verse 22 takes the invitation to draw near the throne a step closer than the earlier verse. Describe the condition of the heart God invites

to come near.

_____

_____

I LISTEN

There are times when it seems that a look into the depth of our soul would strengthen our faith. In a way Hebrews 10:22 does this. Can you see Jesus sprinkling His blood on the inner recesses of your heart? Flooding from your life the impurities that would keep you from serving Him with a pure conscience?

God wants to make you His cleansed vessel, "sanctified and useful for the Master, prepared for every good work" (2 Tim. 2:21). Ask Him to prepare you to do His work today. Be ready to receive from Him a specific job. Then do it!

I WORSHIP HIM

When we receive Jesus as our Savior He fills our spirit—the Holy of Holies—with His presence and invites us to come near. No matter where we are we can by faith enter the Holy of Holies.

Do it now.

❧ DAY 2 ❧

GOD SPEAKS

"LET US. . . ."

Read **Hebrews 10:21-25.**

1. Has another believer stimulated you to show love or do good deeds? How did they do it? What did they encourage you to do?

_____

_____

_____

2. Two facts are evident in Hebrews **10:19-21**:
   a. Jesus' blood opens the way into God's presence.
   b. His presence fills our hearts.
   On the basis of these facts we're given three commands (**vv. 22-24**).

   (**v. 22**) Let us _____

   (**v. 23**) Let us _____

   (**v. 23**) Let us _____

3. The theme of drawing near to God is important to God, the writer and to us. God wants us to draw near with a sincere heart. What are some synonyms for *sincere*?

   _____

   The reference to sprinkled hearts and washed bodies is reminiscent of the pure heart Jesus talked about in **Matthew 5:8**. What does a sincere heart and a pure heart have in common?

   _____

4. The second commandment is "Let us _____"
   (**v. 23**). How has the writer previously described *hope* (**Heb. 6:19**)?

   _____

5. The third commandment (**vv. 24-25**), "Let us _____
   and _____." *The Amplified Bible* says, "And let us consider and give attentive, continuous care to watching over one another, studying how we may stir up (stimulate and incite) to love and helpful deeds and noble activities" (Heb. 10:24).

   How has another believer stimulated you to love when you felt unloving?

How can the local church be an arena of encouragement for both you and other believers?

I LISTEN

The three "let us" commandments make a play on words we'll call "Three Lettuce Salad." Ask yourself: Of what ingredients am I in short supply? A pure heart? A hope that endures? A faith that stimulates others to love and good deeds?

God has a never ending supply (His Word) you can dip into to supply your lack. Find a verse or several verses that meet your need. Prayerfully blend them into your heart, then serve them up with love to others. You'll be glad you did.

I WORSHIP HIM

When Jesus was here on earth, He referred to Himself as the Way, the Truth and the Life. Worship Him today as the Way that leads you to His heart.

❦ DAY 3 ❦

GOD SPEAKS

A STUDY IN CONTRASTS

Read Hebrews 10:25-39.

1. It seems significant that the warning to those who willfully turn from the living God is preceded by an exhortation to not forsake the gathering of believers in the local church. How has your church encouraged you to remain faithful in your walk with Jesus?

---

2. Compare **Hebrews 10:26-31** to **10:32-39.**

   In these passages the writer uses contrast as a teaching device. He places two groups of people alongside one another to emphasize certain truth. Both passages are powerful and distinct. Write down your observations on each one and answer the questions:

   Hebrews 10:26-31

   The writer of Hebrews could be considered a New Testament prophet. Every once in a while he breaks out of his teaching mode, looks you in the eye, shakes his finger in your face, and proclaims, "Thus saith the Lord!" He does that in this passage.

   Observations: _____

   _____

   Who is this passage addressed to?

   _____

   What characterizes this particular group of people?

   _____

   What do these individuals most need?

   _____

   Hebrews 10:32-39

   The writer of Hebrews is also a pastor with a sensitive heart. Throughout the book he encourages the Hebrews to persevere, to remain faithful to God and to His Word. He longs for them to grow in spiritual maturity.

   Observations: _____

   _____

   Who is this passage addressed to?

_____

What characterizes this particular group of people?

_____

What do these individuals most need?

_____

I LISTEN

We will be studying these passages in more depth in the next two days. But right now you are invited to stop and ask God what His special message is for you today.

Which of these passages speak most directly to your heart? Are there warnings for you to heed (vv. 26-31)? Do you need to be called to repentance?

Or could it be that you need encouragement (vv. 32-39)? Life can give us some pretty hard kicks and no one enjoys suffering, even if it's suffering for the sake of righteousness. What about you? Do you need to be encouraged to stand firm? To hear the call to endure?

Understanding who you are and what you need will help you in your growth toward spiritual maturity.

I WORSHIP HIM

How has God spoken to you today? As a judge? A God of comfort? The Spirit of Grace? Tell Him your heart. He's waiting.

❦ DAY 4 ❦

GOD SPEAKS

A WARNING FROM GOD'S HEART

Read **Hebrews 10:26-31.**
1. What feelings do the words *desertion* and *abandonment* conjure up inside you? Try to put them into words.

_____

_____

2. You've already written down your observations of this passage.
    Now you're ready to think it through again. The following ques-
    tions will help you.

    The Greek word translated "not forsaking the assembling of
    yourselves together" in the preceding verse (**v. 25**) speaks of
    desertion and abandonment. What connection do you see between
    those who give up on worshiping with other believers and the
    warning that follows?

    _____

    _____

    The writer even includes himself in this warning by using the
    word "we." Why do you think this is so?

    _____

3. The writer of Hebrews has a horror of sin that surfaces in this
    passage in strong statements and vivid word pictures. Look back
    on the observations that you wrote down yesterday. What are
    some of the most significant?

    _____

4. Trampling Christ underfoot (**v. 29**) is a dramatic word picture.
    Considering the sacred blood by which he's been sanctified as
    common is an insult to the Spirit. Sin is more than rebellion or
    breaking the law. William Barclay calls it "the wounding of
    love." What would you call it?

    _____

5. The first quotation in verse 30 is from the Song of Moses, which

was sung in the worship services of the early church. The second is also from that song and the book of Psalms (**Deut. 32:35-36, Ps. 135:14**). What is the writer emphasizing about God in these verses?

_____

What is he emphasizing in **verse 31**?

_____

6. Living a life of intentional sin has terrifying consequences. It is a recurring theme that keeps surfacing and resurfacing in Hebrews. You may want to review Day 3, Lesson 2, also the following verses:
   Hebrews 3:12, 4:1, 4:11, 6:4-6
   It appears that the person who purposely grieves God can pass the place where he can be brought back to repentance. Look up **1 John 5:16-17**. Do you think the sin that leads to the physical death referred to here is similar to what the writer to the Hebrews is describing in these verses? Why or why not?

_____

_____

I LISTEN

The writer of Hebrews says it is a dreadful thing for an unrepentant person to fall into the hands of the living God. But it is never a fearful thing for the repentant sinner to fall into the hands of the Savior.

Read one of the Gospel accounts of the crucifixion and Psalm 22:14-18. Jesus' arms were open wide that day—so were His hands.

You can trust your life in the pierced hands of the One Who loves you that much. Tell Him so.

I WORSHIP HIM

The God of mercy and compassion is also a God of consuming fire (Heb. 12:29)—a God with power to remove our impurities and make us into instruments of light. Worship Him now in the beauty and brightness of His holiness (Ps. 96:9).

❦ DAY 5 ❦

GOD SPEAKS

THOSE WHO STAND FIRM

1. Times of suffering are indelibly fixed in a person's memory. Tell about a time when you faced hardship, perhaps even persecution.

    _____

    _____

    _____

Read **Hebrews 10:32-34**.
2. Memories must have surfaced in the minds of the Hebrew Christians when they heard, "But recall the former days. . . . " (vv. 32-34). The moment they'd received the light of salvation they'd faced hostility. List the phrases that would have reminded them of what they'd gone through.

    _____

    _____

    We also discover something the writer himself has experienced. What is it?

    _____

    Look over the things you've listed. Put a star by those you've experienced or can identify with in some way.
    What was it the writer wanted to remind them that they had in **verse 34**?

    _____

Getting to Know the Heart of God

Read **Hebrews 10:35-36.**

3. The word *Therefore* takes the readers from the past into the present (v. 35). What are they being encouraged to do?

_____

4. When the writer exhorts them to persevere by doing the will of God, what comes into your mind (v. 36)?

_____

_____

Earlier this week we studied **Hebrews 10:7-10**. Read those verses and v. 36, then finish these sentences: "Jesus perfectly fulfilled God's will through _____." "When I perservere in faithfulness to God's will, I will _____ _____."

Read **Hebrews 10:37-39.**

5. One of the greatest encouragements we have to continue on is found in the verses quoted from Habakkuk. The writer has taken the prophet's words (Hab. 2:3-4) and applied them to the Messiah (Heb. 10: 37-38). *Jesus is coming!* The writer makes it personal. *The one who lives by faith will not draw away from Him at His coming.*

What about you? What group are you in? Those who draw back? Those who believe? Paraphrase Hebrews 10:39 in your own words. Better yet, make it into a personal prayer.

_____

_____

Challenge Activity: One of the best ways for us to continue on is to remember. Look back over the first ten chapters of Hebrews. In chapters 1-4 we saw Jesus Christ as superior to prophets, angels and even Moses. In chapters 5-10 we saw Him as the superior High Priest who became the superior sacrifice—the Lamb of God who takes away the sin of the world.

How do these truths deepen your understanding of the heart of God? How do they strengthen your faith? Write about it in a letter to a friend. Sharing your heart with her can be a part of sharing your heart with your best friend—the Lord Jesus Christ.

I LISTEN

Hebrews 10 closes with an affirmation of faith. But it is really a beginning. Faith is action. Write a personal testimony of faith in your journal. Be sure to include where you are right now in your journey toward spiritual maturity.

I WORSHIP HIM

Jesus is our Great High Priest—forever. That Jesus fulfilled the duties of the High Priest in Israel and continues to fulfill them is at the very heart of Hebrews. Take a moment now and meditate on the following truths that appear and reappear throughout this majestic book:

- Jesus offered himself "once for all," as the perfect sacrifice for sin.
- Jesus "ever lives to make intercession for them" who "come unto God by Him."
- Jesus is seated "on the right hand of the Majesty on high" to deal gently and patiently with His blood-bought children.

How do these truths make you feel? Express those feelings in a prayer of worship addressed to Jesus, your forever priest.

WALKING ALONG TOGETHER

There's been a wall growing around my heart these past few weeks and I know why. I've been hurt and I've been hurt badly. Some of the ones I love most—my brothers and sisters at the church my husband and I served for 18 years—have turned against us.

I don't ever want to go to church again. I want to bury myself away from everyone. Maybe then the pain will go away. . . .

A Message from My Lord

"Let us not give up meeting together, as some are in the habit of doing. . . . " (Heb. 10:25 NIV). The shock of those word are like ice water on the back of my neck.

135

Getting to Know the Heart of God

I continue reading. The message is for me—forsaking the church can lead to rejecting my Lord. Trampling "the Son of God under foot," insulting "the Spirit of grace," "It is a dreadful thing to fall into the hands of the living God." The words don't stop. "Remember those earlier days. . . ."

Yes, I remember.

Perseverance, endurance, steadfastness—this is an area my Lord has stressed for me over a long period of time. As I look back over my life and into the depths of who I am, I see a pattern.

My deepest childhood fear was always fear of failure, so I rarely tried anything new. It was hard for me to finish what I started—I'd clear the kitchen table and forget to wipe off the toast crumbs. I'd start to straighten the books in the bookcase only to be discovered hours later sitting in the corner, books piled around me, leisurely leafing through a volume.

When I was in my teens a family friend noted, "Eva doesn't have any backbone." As an adult I've struggled with following through on hard things. Often I'm tempted to give up, run away or withdraw.

But I'm learning—I'm listening to the Lord's voice and gradually I'm seeing that perseverence and endurance are an important part of growing in spiritual maturity. Gradually I'm seeing my greatest weakness being transformed into my greatest strength.

Except now.

A Flower that Endures

I want to record what I'm learning in my journal. I open my notebook—an old picture I cut from a magazine years ago falls into my hands. A white mountain flower with bits of red blush pushes up through ice-encrusted snow. It's fragile but determined, risking cold and harsh surroundings to bloom in simple pure beauty right where it's been planted.

I reach out and touch the bits of silver ice flecking its tender blossoms. *Endurance, perseverance.*

I trace the tiny red blush close to its heart. *Therefore remember. . . .* "do not cast away your confidence," "For yet a little while, and He who is coming will come. . . ."

Expectantly Waiting

The writer of Hebrews spoke of Jesus' return in chapter nine as

136

well as in ten. "So Christ also, having been offered once to bear the sins of many, shall appear a second time for salvation without reference to sin, to those who eagerly await Him" (Heb. 9:28 NASB).

"Those who eagerly wait for Him." The Israelites eagerly waited outside the tent for their high priest to reappear. They even tied bells to his garments to reassure them that he was still alive while he was inside the Holy Place. A rope was tied around his waist in case he didn't return and they had to pull him out. I can picture them standing there with bated breath. They can hardly wait for his appearance.

No wonder the writer who so loved contrasts would compare our waiting for Christ to those waiting outside the tabernacle.

My wonderings turn into a prayer. *"Lord, teach me to wait, to eagerly anticipate Your return. I know that part of my eager waiting is coming into Your presence. But it's also an expectant waiting that has to do with writing, teaching . . . and yes, being cleansed to serve Your Body, the church of the living God."*

I reach for the *Letter to the Hebrews* by William Barclay. There's a quotation there I don't want to forget. I marked it in red.

> The sacrifice of Jesus perfectly shows the love of God. In that life of service and in that death of love, there stands fully displayed the heart of God. Looking at Jesus, we can say: "That is what God is like."[2]

"Lord Jesus, teach me to trust again. To persevere. To serve Your church, Your Body, in such a way that it reveals to people the heart of God."

I look at my flower picture. Almost I wish I could push aside the icy particles. But if I did, the white of the petals wouldn't reflect the glow of snow. Nor would the crimson in its heart shine as brightly. *Holiness, faithfulness, endurance, the sacrifice of a life poured out for others.*

Therefore remember. . . .

"You need to persevere so that when you have done the will of God, you will receive what he has promised. For in just a very little while, 'he who is coming will come and will not delay'" (Heb. 10:36-37 NIV).

"Lord, I'm waiting."

Source Notes

CHAPTER 1

1. Louis T. Talbot, *Christ in the Tabernacle* (Wheaton, IL: Van Kampen Press, 1942), p. 9.
2. *NIV Study Bible* (Grand Rapids, MI: Zondervan Corporation, 1986), p. 1861.
3. William Barclay, *The Letter to the Hebrews, Revised Edition* (Philadelphia, PA: Westminster Press, 1976), p. 31.
4. *NIV Study Bible*, p. 1864.

CHAPTER 2

1. Charles R. Swindoll, *The Preeminence of Christ* (Fullerton, CA: Insight for Living, 1983), p. 97.
2. *The NIV Study Bible*, p. 1864.
3. *Bible Knowledge Commentary* (Wheaton, IL: Victor Books, A Division of Scripture Press Publications, Inc., 1983), p. 794.
4. Barclay, pp. 50, 59.

CHAPTER 3

1. *NIV Study Bible*, p. 1865.

CHAPTER 4

1. Simon J. Kistemaker, *New Testament Commentary: Hebrews* (Grand Rapids, MI: Baker Book House Company, 1986), p. 200.
2. William Barclay, *The Letter to the Hebrews* (Edinburgh, Scotland: The Saint Andrew Press, 1957), p. 85.

CHAPTER 5

1. Kistemaker, p. 216.
2. William Barclay, *The Letter to the Hebrews, Revised Edition*, p. 92.
3. Swindoll, p. 133.
4. *The Holy Bible, The New King James Version, Prophecy Edition* (Nashville, TN: Thomas Nelson, Inc., 1985), p. 1178.

CHAPTER 6

1. William Barclay, *The Letter to the Hebrews, Revised Edition*, pp. 94, 95.
2. *The New Scofield Reference Bible* (New York: Oxford University Press, Inc., 1967), p. 104.

CHAPTER 7

1. William Barclay, *The Letter to the Hebrews, Revised Edition*, p. 108.
2. Charles R. Swindoll, *Hebrews, Volume I* (Fullerton, CA: Insight for Living, 1983), p. 82.

CHAPTER 8

1. Kistemaker, p. 207.
2. William Barclay, *The Letter to the Hebrews, Revised Edition*, p. 117.

How to Receive a Leader's Guide for
Getting to Know the Heart of God, Hebrews, Chapters 5-10

If God is calling you to lead this study, we have a treat for you! Author Eva Gibson has written another special *Leader's Guide* for Hebrews, Chapter 5-10, especially for Aglow women. We want you to have it as our gift (you pay only postage and handling) with our thanks for being a faithful servant/leader of His Word.

Here are five easy steps:

1. Please complete the information on the next page.
2. Cut along the dotted line.
3. Enclose a 6" x 9" self-addressed envelope, in order to mail the guide back to you.
4. If you live in the U.S. or Canada, enclose a check or money order for $1 **PER COPY** made out to W.A.F.I.* (Overseas, $2.50 U.S.) Do not send cash.
5. Mail: (1) the Bible study request form, (2) your check or money order, (3) self-addressed 6" x 9" envelope to

Bible Study Editor
AGLOW
P.O. BOX 1548
LYNNWOOD, WA 98046-1548
USA

God bless you as you help the Word to go forth.

Once you have completed the study, we would appreciate your constructive ideas by filling in our questionnaire on the next pages and mailing it to us.

*If your fellowship is leading more than one study, you have our blessing to photocopy the *Leader's Guide* as your needs dictate.

Request for Leader's Guide for
Getting to Know the Heart of God, **Hebrews, Chapters 5-10**

PLEASE PRINT OR TYPE

Name _____

Address _____

City, State, Zip _____

Phone (_____)_____

Send me _____ copies of the *Leader's Guide* for *Hebrews, Chapters 5-10.*

I have enclosed _____ to cover the mailing cost of _____ copies of the *Leader's Guide.*

DATE_____

We Value Your Input on
Getting to Know the Heart of God, Hebrews, Chapters 5-10

Since this Bible study is the second of a new series in a new format, we would appreciate your input. We want to know your comments and concerns. When you have filled out this short questionnaire, please cut at the indicated line and mail back to us: Women's Aglow Fellowship International, Attn: Marketing Manager, P.O. Box 1548, Lynnwood, WA 98046-1548, U.S.A.

1. What made you buy this Bible study? (please mark only one)
   ❏ I have wanted a new Bible study from Aglow for a long time
   ❏ The topic interested me
   ❏ Nice cover
   ❏ Someone recommended it
   ❏ Other (please specify) _____

2. Did this Bible study meet or exceed your expectations?
   ❏ Yes (go to question 4)
   ❏ No (go to question 3)

3. Why did this Bible study not meet your expectations? (please mark only **ONE**)
   ❏ Didn't like the content
   ❏ Didn't like the format/lessons
   ❏ Didn't like the cover
   ❏ The lessons were not in-depth/thorough enough
   ❏ The lessons were too in-depth/advanced
   ❏ Each lesson was too time consuming
   ❏ Other (please specify) _____

4. What did you like most about this Bible study? (please mark only one)
   ❏ The content
   ❏ The format/lessons
   ❏ The cover
   ❏ Other (please specify) _____

5. Please list any comments, ideas, or concerns you might have regarding this second Bible study on Hebrews or our new Bible study series, *Discovering the Heart of God*. Use more paper if you wish.

6. Did you purchase this Bible study for use in a group or for individual study? (Please mark only one.)
   ❐ For use in Aglow group
   ❐ For use in church group
   ❐ Individual study
   ❐ Both group and individual study

7. What is the age range of the people using this study?
   ❐ 15-25
   ❐ 26-35
   ❐ 36-45
   ❐ 46-55
   ❐ 56-65
   ❐ 66-75
   ❐ 76+

8. Are you a group leader?
   ❐ Yes
   ❐ No

Thank you for taking the time to fill out this questionnaire and helping us to serve you better.

(10/94)